Breaking Free From Codependency

Mastering the Art of Healthy Boundaries, Building Emotional Intelligence, and Ending the People-Pleasing Cycle

Cameron J. Clark

Table of Contents

INTRODUCTION 1

CHAPTER 1: A CHILD'S FIRST LOVE 5

UNDERSTANDING THE SACRED BOND BETWEEN A MOTHER AND CHILD . 5
Still Face Experiment.. 7
The Opposite of Still Face 9
ATTACHMENT THEORY 12
Secure Attachment 14
Avoidant Attachment 15
Disorganized Attachment 18
Anxious Attachment 21

CHAPTER 2: WHAT IS CODEPENDENCY? 25

DEFINING CODEPENDENCY 25
Codependency and Personality Disorders........................... 30
Myths About Codependency... 33
CODEPENDENCY AND CHILDHOOD EMOTIONAL NEGLECT 36

CHAPTER 3: SURVIVING THE TRAUMATIC CHILDHOOD YEARS 41

THE DIFFERENT FACES OF CODEPENDENCY 41
Substance Abuse.. 42
Emotional Abuse.. 48
Overprotective or Permissive Parenting 52

CHAPTER 4: EARLY SIGNS OF IDENTITY ISSUES 59

HOW BEING RAISED IN A DYSFUNCTIONAL FAMILY AFFECTS YOUR IDENTITY.. 59
WHAT DOES IT MEAN TO HAVE A SOLID SENSE OF SELF? 62
Three Critical Identity Developments.................................. 63
THE CONSEQUENCES OF HAVING AN UNSTABLE SENSE OF SELF 67

CHAPTER 5: GOING BEYOND PEOPLE-PLEASING 71

HOW CODEPENDENCY AFFECTS YOUR SELF-WORTH 71
Weak or Rigid Boundaries 73
Comparing Yourself to Others 77
The Need for Excessive Control 79
EXERCISES TO REBUILD SELF-WORTH 81
Journal Exercise 1: How Well Do You Understand Yourself? 83
Journal Exercise 2: How Much Do You Accept Yourself? . 85
Journal Exercise 3: How Much Do You Love Yourself? 86

CHAPTER 6: BREAKING THE CYCLE OF CODEPENDENCY 91

WHAT ARE THE STAGES OF CODEPENDENCY? 91
Early Stage 92
Middle Stage 93
Late Stage 94
INTERVENTIONS TO BREAK THE CYCLE OF CODEPENDENCY 95
Cognitive Behavioral Therapy 95
Codependents Anonymous 97
Loving Detachment 100

CHAPTER 7: HEALING BEGINS WITH ACCEPTANCE 107

TAKE THE FIRST STEP 107
CONFRONT THE SHADOW 109
Steps to Practice Shadow Work 111
NURTURE YOUR INNER CHILD 115
Be the Parent You Wish You Had 119

CHAPTER 8: BREAK FREE FROM CODEPENDENT LOVING RELATIONSHIPS 127

WHAT DO CODEPENDENT FRIENDSHIPS AND ROMANTIC RELATIONSHIPS LOOK LIKE? 127
What's in It for You? 130
Strategies to Break Free From Codependent Friendships and Romantic Relationships 131

CHAPTER 9: BREAK FREE FROM CODEPENDENT WORK RELATIONSHIPS 139

WHAT DO CODEPENDENT WORK RELATIONSHIPS LOOK LIKE? 139
   What About Codependent Managers? *141*
   Strategies to Break Free From Codependent Work
   Relationships *142*

CONCLUSION **147**

ABOUT THE AUTHOR **149**

REFERENCES **151**

Introduction

Many of us live in denial of who we truly are because we fear losing someone or something—and there are times that if we don't rock the boat, too often the one we lose is ourselves. –Dennis Merritt Jones

From the moment you were born, you had a need for relationships. This is a core need that every human being is born with. Relationships offer an opportunity to be seen and validated by others—two important emotional needs that help you build a stable sense of self and find your place in the world.

However, little did you know that you would spend the rest of your life learning how to build and maintain healthy relationships. Perhaps if you were raised in a stable and reassuring environment, you wouldn't find yourself alternating between yearning for love and being deathly afraid of it so often. And certainly, you wouldn't display signs of a dysfunctional relationship pattern known as codependency.

Codependency can be defined as a learned behavior that stems from early childhood relationships where your vital needs (i.e. the needs for safety, stability, and affection) were unmet. It is often displayed through patterns of people-pleasing, clinginess, fear of abandonment, or the merging of identities with the other person.

Pop culture tends to depict codependency differently, choosing to portray it as a sacrificial type of love—something that friends, family members, and couples should aim for. The idea of loving someone to the extent of forgetting who you are or spending every minute of the day texting them is seen as the ultimate expression of devotion.

Musicians have written songs about codependency, poeticizing the enmeshment between two people. For example, in their duet, "No Air," musicians Jordin Sparks and Chris Brown sing about the fear of separation that is the bedrock of codependency (Sparks & Brown, 2008):

> *But how do you expect me*
>
> *To live alone with just me?*
>
> *'Cause my world revolves around you*
>
> *It's so hard for me to breathe*

In another love song titled "Issues," Julia Michaels sings about the enabling and lack of boundaries that exists in codependent relationships (Michaels, 2017):

> *'Cause I got issues, but you got 'em too*
>
> *So give 'em all to me, and I'll give mine to you*
>
> *Bask in the glory of all our problems*

'Cause we got the kind of love it takes to solve 'em

The truth of the matter is that neither the fear of separation nor the lack of boundaries is beneficial for building long-lasting, reciprocal, and loving relationships. Codependency is a demoralizing and self-destructive behavior that limits your capacity to truly accept yourself and others for who they are. Instead of entering relationships with the purpose of sharing, building, or growing, codependency causes you to be drawn to people who need you.

The aim of this book is to shatter the myths around codependency, such as it being a mental illness or a relationship dynamic that only affects women who are raised by or partnered with addicts. The reality is that codependency can occur in any type of relationship where there is a giver and a taker. This one-sided relationship doesn't need to be romantic either, as this dynamic can be seen between parents and children, best friends, or coworkers.

The book will also explore self-healing therapies like shadow work and inner child healing, which are the attachment issues developed during childhood, to help you get down to the root of codependency. You will learn various ways to begin healing childhood trauma by identifying unmet emotional needs and becoming your own source of strength. Even though you cannot physically turn back time and fix your childhood, you can choose to break free from codependent relationships.

If nobody has told you this before, hear me when I say that there is nothing wrong with you. You are not emotionally weaker just because you give all of yourself to others. In fact, being so compassionate toward others after having been mistreated in the past shows that you are a resilient human being.

Nonetheless, giving your all in one-sided relationships, where the same pattern occurred and you got hurt at the end, will only trigger past rejection and abandonment wounds. Therefore, it is important to develop emotional intelligence and healthy boundaries, which can help you identify takers from those who actually have your best interests at heart and desire to respond to your needs. The following chapters will provide useful information to help you get started in breaking free from codependency!

Chapter 1:

A Child's First Love

The mother's heart is the child's schoolroom. –Henry Ward Beecher

Understanding the Sacred Bond Between a Mother and Child

An attachment is a deep connection that is developed between a primary caregiver and their child. For many years, researchers believed that an attachment was established within the first days and weeks of a child's life, but studies suggest that the bond begins inside the womb (Pregnancy, Birth, and Baby, 2023).

There is a level of consciousness that a growing baby has, which makes it aware of sounds, sights, language, and sensations. However, it isn't the same kind of sensory awareness that a child outside the womb would experience. Everything that the baby senses comes from information passed through the placenta, via the mother's bloodstream. This means that whatever the mother feels physically or psychologically, the baby senses, too.

The mother and baby can either bond over healthy chemicals and hormones or unhealthy, stress-induced chemicals and hormones. This has a lot to do with the type of environment and stressors the mother is exposed to during pregnancy. One study showed that severe stress or anxiety during pregnancy can negatively impact the environment inside the womb, increasing the risks of preterm labor and health complications after the baby is born (March of Dimes, 2023). Chronic stress was also linked to impairments to the baby's brain development, which predicted cognitive and behavioral challenges after birth.

Another study showed that babies were more likely to show signs of slow or impaired development when the mother's psychological state was inconsistent from the time of pregnancy to life outside of the womb (Association for Psychological Science, 2011). For example, babies whose mothers were either healthy during and after pregnancy or depressed during and after pregnancy showed positive signs of development. However, those whose mothers started out healthy but became depressed, or vice versa, showed signs of slow development (Association for Psychological Science, 2011). The change in conditions made it difficult for the child to regain their bearing.

This sacred bond between mother and child affects the child more than it does the mother. For instance, the feeling of stress is something the mother has felt many times in the past, especially if they have grown up in adverse circumstances or have been exposed to abusive relationships. However, the growing baby is experiencing stress for the first time—and the worst part is that it is coming from someone whom their survival depends on.

Even before the child is born, they already have a volatile relationship with their mother and, subsequently, with the world. They are sensitive to her fluctuating moods and ongoing stress, which influences how they think, feel, and behave. In some cases, the mother's unstable mental and emotional well-being can create permanent cognitive or behavioral struggles that the child will have to live with for the rest of their life. This first impression made inside the womb will also impact the attachment formed outside the womb.

Still Face Experiment

The famous psychological experiment known as the "still face" experiment was invented by Dr. Ed Tronick in the 1970s (Gregory, 2019). The aim of the experiment was to investigate the significance of the parent-child bond and how that might positively or negatively affect the child's physical, cognitive, emotional, and social development. In particular, the researcher wanted to determine how an emotionless parent can affect a child's sense of security.

The experiment starts out with a mother sitting across from her child, smiling and playing with them. She is emotionally responsive to her child's needs and creates a mutually satisfying exchange. Then suddenly, the mother displays a still face for two minutes. At that point, the researcher observed a few physical and emotional changes in the child's behavior. They would test their mother's emotional responsiveness by being playful, but when they received a blank face in response, the child would move around frantically, showing physical signs of distress.

The longer the mother went without showing emotion, the more overwhelmed the child would become. One particular child during the experiment tried to self-soothe by biting her hand, while others cried and screeched. Toward the end of the two minutes of still face, the child would become tired, withdrawn, and distracted by something else in the room. At this stage, they were hopeless about reconnecting with their mother. When the mother returned to her normal happy disposition, the child would show a visible sense of relief and resume playing.

Even though this is a short experiment, it gives parents a glimpse of how long-term emotional unavailability affects children. Unresponsiveness, such as when parents are distracted, withdrawn, or unmoved by their children, causes emotional distress and, over time, this may impact their children's development. Of course, these dire consequences don't occur overnight. Since children are resilient, it would take more than a couple of missed opportunities for connection before any serious developmental problems start to show.

It is also worth pointing out that not every child is at risk of being raised by unresponsive parents. In general, parents who are more likely to struggle with unresponsiveness are those who are living with an injury or illness, are a victim of domestic abuse, suffer from anxiety or mood disorders, or battle with substance abuse. Other types of addictions that may cause parents to be emotionally unresponsive are working excessively, gambling, or being preoccupied with their phones.

Think back to the discussion about the attachment between a mother and child that starts in the womb. Imagine the type of pregnancy an overwhelmed or emotionally unstable mother-to-be might have and how they would bond with their child after birth. Try to picture how they would respond to their child's cries for physical and emotional needs. Being a mother is already one of the most demanding jobs in the world, but it comes with added stress when you are mentally unhealthy.

Poor mental health robs many mothers of the joys of parenthood, like nurturing a little human. Mental illness, abuse, and other factors already mentioned cause mothers to become so preoccupied with their own survival or well-being that they become neglectful of their children. Small inconveniences and sacrifices that come with parenting might cause them to shut down, have meltdowns, or isolate themselves, leaving the child to self-regulate on their own.

The Opposite of Still Face

You may be wondering what the opposite of unresponsiveness looks like. Is it an extremely positive mother who coddles their child and does everything in her power to make sure the child is safe and happy? Not quite. The opposite of unresponsive is a mother who returns most (not all) of her child's bids for connection.

The concept of bids was made popular by American psychologist John Gottman. His findings, after 40 years of conducting research, revealed that emotional connection between two people was strengthened when both parties were sensitive and responsive to each other's bids for connection. He defines a bid as a gesture to get attention, affection, and acceptance from a loved one (Eanes, 2016). Since this is a form of indirect communication, many bids are often ignored.

For a newborn baby, their way of attempting to get attention, affection, and acceptance may be to cry, whine, smile, or laugh. Due to the lack of speaking abilities or knowledge of social cues, they will most likely use the same handful of gestures to make bids. Older children may be able to make bids by letting out a big sigh (i.e., a bid for their parents to ask how they are feeling) or asking general knowledge questions (i.e., a bid for their parents to give them attention). To unassuming parents who aren't aware that these are bids, they can see their children as being needy, bored, or irritating.

In the still face experiment, the mothers were forced to ignore their children's bids for connection by appearing withdrawn. After a few minutes of unresponsiveness, the children showed frustration, then stopped making bids completely. The same experience is witnessed in real life. After a child makes several bids for connection without getting the appropriate reaction from their parents, they stop making bids altogether. They don't necessarily "shut down" in the same way an adult would, but they simply stop expecting that kind of emotional responsiveness from their parents. They may even forget that they have a need for attention, affection, and acceptance until they grow up and observe their peculiar interactions with others.

For example, a little girl whose mother failed to respond to most of their bids for connection may grow up to be a young woman who fears closeness in relationships. The first few stages of getting to know someone new may go smoothly, but as soon as the relationship starts to require vulnerability, they may withdraw. The reason for this is because as a child, their emotions were not validated or given the chance to be explored and expressed in a safe environment. Being vulnerable is unfamiliar to them and could possibly be interpreted as a threat or weakness.

When it comes to responding to bids, quality matters more than quantity. Think about the memories you still hold from childhood. Do you remember every interaction with your parents or just the ones that were heartfelt and made you feel unquestionably loved by them? Parents are not perfect people. Before they had children, they were normal adults trying to process their own traumas and make something out of their lives.

Parents are not expected to never have bad days, curse in front of their children, or display signs of stress and anxiety. Even the most loving parents will slip up and miss some bids for connection. However, if it is a constant pattern of failing to respond to bids, then children may interpret the unresponsiveness as a sign of rejection. Therefore, instead of focusing on responding to every bid, parents should show up when it counts the most. Some of the loving behaviors that leave a positive imprint on children's minds include

- listening attentively when they are speaking
- validating their strong emotions
- showing interest in what they care about
- bonding over playful activities
- offering hugs and kisses when they feel upset
- showing enthusiasm when you haven't seen them in a while

Before moving on to the next section about attachment styles, reflect on your childhood and how often your bids for connection were acknowledged. Would you say you had parents who were responsive or unresponsive, and what behaviors gave that away?

Attachment Theory

Babies and small children aren't mature enough to grasp the concept of "love." All they understand is attachment. The quality of the attachment formed with parents determines how safe children feel exploring the world and developing a sense of self. The closest expression of love that children recognize is providing a home environment that is nurturing.

Parents, on the other hand, have some level of understanding about what love means. They, too, were once children who formed attachments with their parents and grew up to build personal and professional relationships with others. Unlike their little ones, parents are capable of expressing love in different ways by responding to their children's needs for attention, affection, and acceptance.

Nonetheless, we know from our own experiences that not every parent displays love to a child. It isn't that they don't know what love is but that they find it difficult to express it. Some parents who attempt to show love to their children end up hurting them rather than building them up. For example, they might express a transactional love (e.g. rewarding children with love for good behavior) or a controlling love (e.g. undermining their children's ability to form a separate identity to the parent).

What's important to emphasize is that parents' challenges showing love have nothing to do with their children. They date back to childhood or past abusive relationships where they were denied the opportunity to receive genuine love. Children simply act as mirrors, reflecting back to parents their own issues with intimacy and vulnerability. The sad reality is that children are too young to understand it is not their fault that their parents are cold, distant, inconsistent, or withdrawn from them. The challenges that their parents have with love existed before they were even born—and subsequently continue afterward.

The attachment theory, founded by John Bowlby and expanded by Mary Ainsworth, seeks to explain how early childhood attachment affects the parent-child relationship as well as how children develop a sense of self. In essence, this theory outlines the consequences of conditional, inconsistent, or nonexistent love in parent-child relationships. Once again, since children are too young to understand what love is, they cannot be expected to take the lead and show love to their parents. It is the duty of parents to step out of themselves and show unconditional love to their children.

Secure Attachment

According to the theory, there are four styles of attachment. The ideal type of attachment is called secure attachment. It is typically formed when parents are conscious of how their behaviors affect children and seek to create a reassuring environment where children are allowed to express themselves freely. Of course, these relationships are built on structure and boundaries; however, parents are willing to listen and validate the needs of their children and negotiate conditions when required. As a result, children feel respected and accepted by their parents, which gives them the confidence to assert themselves in other relationships.

Below are the signs that children have developed a secure attachment with their parents:

- ability to regulate strong emotions

- easily build relationships and trust others

- ability to articulate their thoughts and feelings

- manage conflict with confidence; seeking win-win situations

- ability to empathize with others and be present in relationships

- high self-esteem; do not define themselves by what others think

- ability to self-reflect and correct troublesome behaviors

- positively receive constructive criticism and offer others fair feedback

These children end up becoming adults who are at peace with themselves and others. Certainly, their relationships won't be perfect, but they have the emotional skills to solve interpersonal problems and maintain harmony with others. They believe in true love and may seek meaningful relationships because of being shown unconditional love as children.

Avoidant Attachment

The remaining three styles of attachment reflect unstable parent-child relationships where love is either not given at all or given intermittently. The first of these styles of attachment is called avoidant attachment (also known as dismissive-avoidant and anxious-avoidant attachment). It typically develops when parents have trouble displaying physical and emotional intimacy. They put up an imaginary wall between them and their children and relate from a distance. Children sense that they cannot fully reach and engage with their parents due to constantly running into a wall.

Eventually, children stop trying to connect with their parents emotionally because of the rejection they face whenever they do. Instead they find other ways to bond with their parents that may not require emotional intimacy. For example, if a parent takes education seriously, their child may seek to bond with them by getting good grades at school. They notice how happy this behavior makes their parents and decide to continue excelling at school. This type of transactional love becomes a substitute for real connection, which the child is comfortable with—until they grow up and recognize that transactional love is empty and cannot fulfill the longing for genuine acceptance.

As adults, children raised by avoidant parents can become avoidant adults, too. For example, the same preoccupations that may have caused their parents to stay away from home or seem disinterested become their obsessions and preoccupations, too. They are also more likely to fall into different forms of addiction, such as substance abuse, eating disorders, or living a promiscuous lifestyle because of their tendency to avoid dealing with emotional stress and instead seek outlets to run and hide.

Some of the tell-tale signs that an adult has an avoidant personality include

- pulling away from relationships when they get too personal

- shutting down emotionally when faced with stressful situations

- feeling uncomfortable when asked to express their needs

- becoming overly independent and avoiding seeking help from others

- chasing goals to prove something rather than doing what they love

- being skeptical of people who are too emotional or overshare

- having commitment issues; preferring relationships that don't demand too much from them

Avoidant parents can come across like they are always angry, irritable, or triggered by something. Many of them are still attempting to process complex trauma while simultaneously managing adult responsibilities. Life can be very overwhelming for them; however, since they are uncomfortable showing vulnerability or asking for help, they project their strong feelings to everyone around them.

Children bear the brunt of their parents' psychological distress and may grow up feeling guilty or responsible for not making their parents' lives easier or more manageable. But once again, these psychological issues existed long before they were born; therefore, it is not their fault nor should they feel responsible for healing their parents.

When it comes to defining love, children raised with avoidant attachment can have doubts about whether unconditional love exists. They have seen too many instances from childhood where love came at a cost. As a result, they may grow up to become adults who avoid serious, long-term relationships or battle with trust and control issues when they do enter relationships.

It is also common for them to repeat the same transactional patterns of showing love. For instance, they may believe that the only way to receive love is to "buy it" through gifts, acts of service, support, and anything else their partner may need. The irony, however, is that even when they have "earned" love, they are unable to receive it. There may still be an imaginary wall keeping them from fully trusting and being emotionally available in relationships.

Disorganized Attachment

The second unhealthy attachment is called disorganized attachment (also known as anxious-disorganized attachment). It develops when children are exposed to abuse, neglect, or trauma at a very young age. In most cases, their parents are abusive, mentally ill, or battle with addiction. Children learn to fear their parents due to them having anger issues, being violent, or behaving in unpredictable ways. Their family life is also dysfunctional, meaning that parents don't act like parents and children are forced to grow up too soon.

Disorganized attachment causes children to feel confused about their place within the family as well as their place within society. Since they are brought up in a dysfunctional environment, they are not given stability, structure, or healthy boundaries to learn the difference between acceptable and unacceptable behaviors. Furthermore, their parents' mental and emotional unavailability forces them to teach themselves how to relate with others and navigate life.

When disorganized attachment is formed, children come to believe their parents are unreliable and cannot be trusted to provide a safe environment. As a result, they develop coping mechanisms to shield themselves from ongoing stress and anxiety. For example, a child may become emotionally withdrawn, rebellious, or completely dissociated from their reality. In some cases where a child both idolizes and fears their parent, they may adopt a fake persona that allows them to relate to the parent and, in a way, normalize the dysfunctional relationship between them.

An example is the golden child often seen in families with addiction. The child discovers that their giftedness or "good child syndrome" can help them form some type of relationship with their alcoholic parent. Moreover, they come to see that by being gifted, they can distract the family from the chaos created by the alcoholic parent and bring a sense of hope.

Overtime, the golden child becomes someone who sacrifices their needs to bring peace in the home. When they grow up and realize that the world is just as merciless as their alcoholic parent, they may become resentful for always having to wear a mask to make other people feel good. Many golden children end up falling into addiction, too, or living alternative lifestyles that go against the status quo (another form of rebellion).

Some of the signs that an adult has a disorganized attachment include

- extreme sensitivity to rejection
- difficulty regulating strong emotions
- frequent bouts of anxiety and panic
- difficulty trusting others in relationships
- unexplained mood swings
- engaging in high-risk behaviors

The recurring emotion that adults raised with disorganized attachment feel is fear. They are afraid of anything they cannot control (i.e., anything that creates unpredictability). The need for control can become so debilitating that the only way to relax is to numb the mind with drugs, alcohol, or any other addictive behavior.

Another important thing to consider is that these adults did not receive healthy love as children. In fact, love was seen as something risky and unpredictable. If they do build relationships as adults, they will have a strong need to control their relationships or their partners, in order to feel a sense of safety. We know that love doesn't seek to control; true love encourages others to be themselves.

Anxious Attachment

The third unhealthy attachment (and fourth style of attachment) is anxious attachment (also known as anxious-preoccupied or anxious-ambivalent attachment). It is developed when parents are inconsistent when nurturing their children. They switch between being emotionally available to being absent or neglectful of their children. There is no doubt that these types of parents love their children. The only issue is they aren't able to respond to their children's needs—in the manner that their children require.

A classic example of anxious attachment is a parent who works a lot (or works out of town) and doesn't spend time bonding with their child. Extended family members play more of a supportive role in the child's life, in the absence of their parent. When the parent decides to reunite with the child, they may bring a lot of gifts and shower them with affection, seeking desperately to make up for lost time. But unfortunately, this euphoric feeling is short-lived because after a short while, the parent has to disconnect from their child again and focus on work.

The inconsistent parenting creates an incredible amount of anxiety for the child. While they love their parents very much and seek to connect with them, they are afraid of abrupt abandonment. In response, they could either become needy and clingy, throwing tantrums to get attention from their parents, or they could become withdrawn and choose to hide their true thoughts and feelings to avoid disappointment.

Adults with anxious attachment may come across aloof or standoffish because they need time to get to know people before attaching to them. Due to childhood fears of abandonment, they can have trouble trusting others to show up consistently for them. It is easier for someone with anxious attachment to be the giver than the receiver in a relationship because receiving creates an expectation for someone else to respond to their needs. Being in a position where they depend on others can feel uncomfortable, so they would rather avoid it.

Furthermore, these people tend to hold back showing others their true identity out of fear that being open and vulnerable with others may backfire (e.g., people may be turned off by some of their personality traits). They are also afraid of being too invested in a relationship that may not be sustainable in the long term. As you can tell, the fear of abandonment is one of the underlying motives behind their relationship dynamics. This same fear can also cause the following behaviors:

- alternating from being needy to being detached

- pursuing emotional intimacy then pulling away

- feeling pressure to make relationships work

- being highly sensitive to criticism
- being self-conscious; thinking about how others perceive you
- self-sacrificing in relationships to the point of burnout
- having extreme fear of rejection (real or perceived)
- showing jealousy and possessive tendencies

Adults with anxious attachment are both yearning for true love and deathly afraid of it at the same time. Their early childhood experiences taught them that love could be taken away suddenly. Therefore, as much as they desire closeness, it can be an emotional trigger for them. Nonetheless, there are some adults with anxious attachment who are courageous enough to take the leap of faith and seek intimacy. The only trouble is that they can find themselves being swallowed up in romantic relationships.

Out of the four attachment styles, anxious attachment is the one that is more likely to trigger codependent behaviors. This happens because those with anxious attachments tend to struggle with identity issues, such as low self-esteem, feeling like they aren't worthy of being loved, seeking approval from others, or mirroring the behaviors of others to create closeness. Some of these identity issues may be obvious to them and others may not be.

Relationships become an opportunity to heal insecurities from the past and hopefully receive the unconditional and overflowing love that they yearned for as a child. Since the stakes are so high (i.e., they feel as though they have to make the relationship work), they develop codependent tendencies, such as excessive generosity, clinginess, conflict avoidance, people-pleasing, and control issues.

For the remainder of the book, we will mostly look at various interpersonal problems experienced by people with anxious attachment, with the focus on breaking free from codependency!

Chapter 2:

What Is Codependency?

Codependency doesn't acknowledge that we actually feel what others are experiencing and want it to stop because it hurts us too.
—Jennifer Elizabeth Moore

Defining Codependency

Codependency is an unhealthy relationship pattern that stems from early childhood attachment issues. It is characterized by a dependency on other people that can compromise boundaries and lead to something known as enmeshment (becoming intertwined with others to the extent of losing touch with who you are).

The term "codependency" was first used by members of the Alcoholics Anonymous community to describe loved ones who were enabling addicts by not setting boundaries within the relationships and being overly committed to taking care of their needs, despite the toxic dynamic that was forming. They found that enabling loved ones were getting an emotional benefit of feeling needed from caring for their addicted family members.

Codependency isn't a medical disorder that one might seek a diagnosis or medication for. Instead, it can be described as an unhealthy learned behavior that prevents individuals from building reciprocal and healthy relationships. One of the terms commonly used to describe codependency is "relationship addiction." This is because codependent people tend to center their well-being around relationships. In other words, if their relationships are prospering, they feel calm and balanced. But when their relationships experience turbulence—which is normal and expected in relationships—they can feel anxious and disoriented.

The preoccupation with relationships can also negatively impact how codependent people view themselves. For example, when codependent people are not on good terms with their loved ones, they can experience emotional distress. Seeing their loved ones hurting can make them feel physical pain, too. They are also prone to internalizing other people's emotions and feeling responsible for making them feel better; this can at times cause them to feel undeserved guilt for setting boundaries and standing up for themselves.

The upside of being connected with others' emotional experiences is that codependent people tend to be intuitive and empathetic. If you journey back into their childhoods, you will find moments where the anxiously attached child learned to become sensitive to and anticipate the needs of their parents. They studied which of their own behaviors made their parents upset and which behaviors led to bonding and closeness. Since bonding and closeness was what they yearned for most, they abandoned parts of themselves that were undesirable to their parents and formed an identity around the parts of themselves their parents adored.

Of course, being so intuitive and empathetic means that codependent people need boundaries; otherwise, they can get carried away inside other people's worlds. Boundaries would help them separate who they are (and what they need) from who others are (and what they might need). However, setting boundaries is usually a skill codependent people learn later in life, upon realizing that their needs matter when building healthy relationships.

What makes codependency unhealthy is that those affected by it become neglectful of their own well-being in attempts to maintain their relationships. Since the behavioral pattern of codependency is rooted in the fear of abandonment, there is an unconscious belief that codependent people adopt, which is that unless they constantly adapt to the needs of others, they won't be given the love they deserve. In other words, in exchange for receiving love, the expectation is to sacrifice their own needs, views, desires, and right to make decisions.

Codependent people believe that showing up as themselves in relationships isn't good enough because there is a risk that how they come across might be upsetting for other people—and who knows what might follow afterward?

Getting someone with codependency to reflect on their relationship pattern and see where they are going wrong isn't always easy. For them, their self-sacrifices could be seen as a form of altruism, which refers to the selfless concern for people. Certainly, codependency does trigger a sense of deep compassion for people, which is a personal strength that codependent people display. However, the difference between altruism and codependency is that altruistic people wouldn't deny their own needs in the process of serving others. They would treat serving others as an extension of who they are (i.e., one of their many personality traits) rather than making serving others a core element of their identity.

Codependent relationships have a unique dynamic. Whether the relationship is between a parent and child, romantic couple, colleagues, or friends, the pair will take on two distinct roles: the giver and taker. The giver is the codependent individual who takes on the sole responsibility of keeping the relationship going. Their ongoing and one-sided investments of time, money, praise, support, and compromise ensure that there is enough stability (and possibly harmony) to maintain the relationship.

The taker is typically an independent (and sometimes avoidant) counterpart who receives the return on investment made by the giver. They can, at times, develop a sense of entitlement or manipulative tendencies due to the power imbalance and always having their needs met, without being expected to reciprocate.

If this relationship is one-sided and the giver doesn't receive a fraction of what they invest into it, what makes them stay? This is a question that codependent people struggle to answer. Even though they are so frustrated with the lack of reciprocation and affection they get from their counterparts, there is still a magnetic pull that keeps them together.

The best way to answer the question is to analyze the attachment between a codependent person and their primary caregiver (in most cases their mother). As children, did the codependent person invest more effort accommodating their mother than their mother invested accommodating them? Was the responsibility to be understanding, forgiving, respectful, and compassionate expected only of the child? Did the mother use their authority to manipulate the child into getting whatever she wanted from him or her? Was the child expected to be obedient despite being mistreated by his or her mother?

All of these questions can help to shed light on why codependent people stay in one-sided and unhealthy relationships. They stay because that is the relationship pattern they were made accustomed to since childhood. From a young age, they were groomed into being a giver and never expecting the same courtesy, respect, and sacrifice in return. If they rejected the role of giver, they would upset their parents and potentially jeopardize the one relationship that meant everything to them.

The same relationship pattern is repeated in adult relationships until, of course, they learn new ways of connecting to others that would not compromise their well-being. With the right kinds of therapy and focus on personal development, breaking free from codependency is possible!

Codependency and Personality Disorders

Codependency is sometimes seen as a symptom of an underlying personality disorder. While it is true that codependent people can be diagnosed with a co-occurring personality disorder, it is possible to be codependent without having any other condition. Below we explore how codependency occurs in people with various personality disorders.

Codependency and Borderline Personality Disorder (BPD)

Borderline personality disorder (BPD) is a condition that creates an unstable self-image. It is typically caused by early childhood trauma where the child was often disorientated and couldn't find a sense of security in their relationships. BPD affects how individuals relate to others and the level of safety they feel in relationships. Similar to codependent people, they need ongoing reassurance to feel secure and subconsciously carry a fear of abandonment.

When they attach to people, they can become enmeshed and give everything to make the relationship work. However, their clinginess and expectations of complete devotion can make their counterparts feel overwhelmed. When people with BPD sense tension or uncertainty in relationships, they behave differently than codependent people. Instead of investing more into the relationship to subdue their anxious feelings, people with BPD pull away and display avoidant tendencies.

Codependency and Narcissistic Personality Disorder (NPD)

Narcissistic personality disorder (NPD) can be described as a condition that creates a preoccupation with self to the extent of inflated one's own self-image. Individuals with NPD face extremely threatening life circumstances, which causes them to bury their true identity beneath a grandiose persona that lacks empathy and needs excessive amounts of admiration to feel stable.

Narcissists can display codependent tendencies, however, not for the same reasons as other codependent people. For instance, a narcissist might attach to a person who can provide a constant supply of praise and positive emotions. The praise puffs up their ego, and the positive emotions help them fill an inner void of emptiness. Moreover, narcissists have emotional needs like anybody else, but they lack the self-awareness to respond to their needs. As a result, they gravitate toward people who are natural caretakers (e.g., codependent people) who don't mind taking on that responsibility.

Codependency and Avoidant Personality Disorder (APD)

Avoidant personality disorder (APD) is a condition that causes an intense fear of rejection and avoidance of social interaction. Individuals who suffer with this condition tend to have past experiences of rejection, humiliation, bullying, or abandonment. APD creates a chronic feeling of not being good enough as well as constantly feeling judged by others. It can, therefore, feel safer for these individuals to self-isolate or become extremely selective about who they allow into their circles.

Since APD reinforces avoidant tendencies, it is very difficult for these individuals to build meaningful relationships. However, when they do forge emotional connections with a select few, they become dependent on those relationships to fulfill their emotional needs. This may cause clinginess, possessiveness, control issues, and seeking constant reassurance from loved ones.

Codependency and Dependent Personality Disorder (DPD)

Dependent personality disorder (DPD) is a condition that causes a dependency on others to take care of physical and emotional needs. Individuals with this condition do not believe that they can make decisions concerning their lives on their own. They may also struggle being apart from others for long periods of time because relationships provide a safety net that allows them to feel secure.

Similar to codependency, people with DPD have a strong fear of abandonment, which could stem from a variety of factors such as being abused or forced to obey authorities as children. However, the difference between DPD and codependency is that codependent people need to be needed, whereas people with DPD believe they need others for security.

Since these personality disorders are similar to codependency, it is common for codependent people to be misdiagnosed with one of the above conditions. Furthermore, codependent people may find themselves drawn toward people with personality disorders due to sharing the same core wound—fear of abandonment.

Myths About Codependency

How codependency is portrayed in the media isn't exactly how it is displayed in real life. Dismantling the myths about codependency can help you learn to identify the pattern when it emerges in relationships and respond with the appropriate strategies.

Here are some of the common myths circulating about codependency.

Myth: Only People Who Come From Families With Addiction Are Affected by Codependency

Originally, codependency was a term used to describe enablers in alcoholic families. However, since then, doctors have been able to identify the same relationship patterns in other types of relational dynamics. For example, your primary caregiver may not have been an alcoholic, but they may have been physically, verbally, or emotionally abusive. Or perhaps your caregiver wasn't abusive but instead suffered from a chronic illness that caused the whole family to prioritize their well-being. Other scenarios that can lead to codependency include physical separation from parents, death of a parent, and irresponsible parents.

Myth: You Either Develop Codependency in Childhood or You Don't at All

Childhood attachment issues are one of the main drivers of codependency, but they certainly aren't the only ones. Codependency can also stem from trauma, poverty, addiction, social inequality, and mental illness. In essence, any adverse past experience that could potentially affect your sense of self and ability to trust others can lead to unhealthy relationship patterns like codependency.

Myth: Codependent People Want to Spend All of Their Time With You

It is common for people to mistake codependency for clinginess, although in reality codependency is more involved than mere clinginess. For example, clinginess can be defined as the need to maintain closeness with others. Some (but not all) codependent people can display signs of clinginess, but it isn't the driving force behind their behavior. What codependent people want more than anything is to feel needed. In other words, they want to take responsibility for other people—to be the one they solely rely on. This may or may not involve clingy tendencies.

Myth: People With Codependency Are Manipulative

Codependent people have trouble communicating their needs or setting boundaries with others. As a result, they tend to develop passive-aggressive behaviors, like giving the silent treatment, telling lies, or being "forgetful" to avoid clear and open communication about how they are feeling. The intention for most codependent people isn't to manipulate others but, rather, to avoid confrontation or explosive reactions. It is more likely that codependent people avoid being direct out of fear of hurting others than doing it as a deliberate way to hurt them.

Myth: Codependent People Can't Sustain Healthy Relationships

It can be a devastating thought for codependent people to think they are incapable of sustaining healthy relationships. Due to naturally being hopeless romantics, they dream of one day overcoming their codependent tendencies and building nurturing and reciprocal relationships with others. With the right interventions and ongoing introspection, codependency can be treated. Of course, every now and again, it is common to be triggered into latching onto others, but being aware of these triggers and knowing what to do when they arise can help to regain clarity.

Look over the five myths again and identify the ones you had previously thought to be true. Consider how believing in those myths affected your perception of codependency and, subsequently, how you perceived yourself. It is important to continue exploring codependency to gain a broader and much deeper understanding of what it is beyond what you read online or hear from other people.

Codependency and Childhood Emotional Neglect

The connection between codependency and the fear of abandonment has already been drawn, but what about the connection between codependency and childhood emotional neglect (CEN)?

CEN can be defined as unresponsiveness to a child's emotional needs, such as their need for attention, validation, support, and affection. It also refers to exposing a child to domestic violence and other forms of abuse without getting them the proper medical attention to address cognitive and emotional problems that may arise. In other words, normalizing chaos and disorder at home can be a type of emotional abuse that negatively impacts a child's well-being, sense of self, and ability to form healthy relationships with others.

A child who develops codependent behaviors later in life experiences moments of closeness and distance with their parents. At unpredictable times, their parents can go from being emotionally available and responsive to their needs to being dismissive and unreachable. The switch between closeness and distance creates an environment of CEN in this type of parent-child relationship that is triggered by the inconsistencies in showing up for the child.

To illustrate how CEN works in a parent-child relationship, consider an example of a five-year-old kid living in a house with an aggressive parent. They may or may not be afraid of their parent's rage, but one thing that is certain is that they are used to it. Since they were born, they witnessed their parent consistently respond to situations with aggression like yelling, spanking, being controlling, and demanding things to be done their way. Even though they secretly wish they could see a more nurturing side to their parent, they have learned to adapt to the aggressive parenting style and protect themselves from the harsh realities of their home life.

The scenario would be different if the aggressive parent suffered from a mental illness like bipolar disorder, which caused frequent mood swings. Without any prior warning, they could go from yelling at their five-year-old child to requesting hugs and wanting to play with them. Or spending an entire day bonding with their family, then isolating themselves the next day and refusing to speak to anyone. Put yourself in the five-year-old's shoes for a few minutes and consider what he or she would think and feel.

This switch from connection to disconnection would cause the child to never fully trust that their parent is capable of responding to their needs. They may even become skeptical of their parent's positive emotions and begin to pull away whenever the parent attempts to get close.

Parents don't always realize that they are breadcrumbing their little ones by showing random acts of love. Indeed not every parent is aware that they are behaving this way; in fact, they may be so wrapped up in their own world that they cannot see the impact of their unstable behaviors. Being breadcrumbed teaches kids to be okay with accepting whatever type of love someone shows them (even if the love is unhealthy), and furthermore, it reinforces the message that they are asking for too much when they desire to be loved correctly in relationships.

One of the consequences of CEN, specifically for codependent people, is that they tend to latch onto anybody that shows real or perceived interest in them, without taking the time to assess whether the connection is genuine and mutual. CEN can also cause codependent people to stay on guard for any signs of their partners pulling away or switching from being close to being distant.

This kind of worry can be stressful and prevent them from actually being present and enjoying the process of getting to know others. Moreover, it can make them self-conscious, such as monitoring how often they speak to their significant other, analyzing how their significant other responds to different behaviors and modifying accordingly, self-correcting or finding passive ways of communicating their needs as well as trying not to do or say anything that might cause their significant other to pull away.

If you would like to examine for yourself how CEN may or may not have played a role in your childhood, take a walk down memory lane and try to identify moments of CEN that left an imprint on you. For example, did you have parents who breadcrumbed you, expressing love intermittently? Were there some obvious cognitive, behavioral, or emotional challenges you had as a child that your parents ignored or downplayed? Or were you raised by a mentally ill parent who couldn't show up for you all of the time due their condition?

Go a step further and consider how CEN could have influenced your perception of love. Put yourself in the shoes of your younger self and try to remember how they understood love. How did they make sense of receiving affection at unpredictable times? For instance, did they believe love was unreliable? Did they feel pressure to meet certain conditions before earning love? Did love cause emotional pain at some point? All of these beliefs about love fuel and give more reasons to justify the development of codependency.

Chapter 3:

Surviving the Traumatic Childhood Years

The more we uncover who we are not and discard our disempowering unconscious behaviors, the more closely we can be in sync with our true, authentic selves. –Christopher Dines

The Different Faces of Codependency

Codependency has different faces, meaning that it doesn't stem from the same psychosocial issues for everyone. Broadening your understanding of codependency can help you show greater empathy to those who may have different life stories from your own but who are also struggling with the same unhealthy relationship pattern.

Another point worth noting is that codependency may not look the same in every relationship. For example, the typical giver and taker dynamic may not be so obvious between an employer and employee due to the nature of their relationship. It is expected for an employee to perform work duties and for the employer to set expectations and provide feedback on their performance. So, how can one tell when this professional relationship has become one-sided?

Codependency can also range from mild to severe, depending on factors like past traumatic history, co-occuring mental health conditions, stress and lifestyle factors, and openness to therapy and other psychological interventions. It is also possible to display codependent tendencies in one type of relationship (e.g., romantic relationships) but build and maintain healthy and nurturing relationships in other aspects of your life.

Can you see how many different faces codependency has? As you read through the following sections about the different causes of codependency, try to imagine different people, from various social and cultural backgrounds, whose unique life circumstances led to the adoption of codependent behaviors.

Substance Abuse

Healthy relationships are about two individuals coming together and creating a safe environment for both of their needs to be met and where their individuality is respected and celebrated. Power is shared between the individuals, and nobody feels more important than the other.

Substance abuse creates the opposite dynamic. The individual with the substance abuse problem tends to have more power in the relationship due to their lack of concern for their counterpart. When sober, their focus is on accessing and using their drug of choice, and when they are intoxicated, they lack the awareness to recognize and respond to their counterpart's needs.

Despite the power imbalance and selfish behaviors, many relationships with substance abuse issues can remain intact for years. However, it is never the individual with the drug or alcohol problem that does the work of keeping the relationship together. Most of the time, it is the codependent partner who will light themselves on fire to keep the relationship warm and comfortable. They will adjust their routines, behaviors, and expectations to make the relationship as functional as possible.

The codependent partner may not even realize how many personal sacrifices they have made since the beginning of the relationship to keep the other person happy. This has a lot to do with learned habits they picked up from childhood, such as going above and beyond to please their parents. As a kid, personal sacrifices needed to be made on an ongoing basis to maintain some sort of normalcy or keep the relationship with their parents cordial.

Years later when they meet someone with a substance abuse problem, they are already familiar with the mood swings, emotional outbursts, manipulation, and other harmful patterns that cause them to forget about themselves and focus on the other person's needs. If they have not healed from their own childhood trauma, they are likely to repeat the same unhealthy relationship patterns formed earlier in life with their parents.

The effects of substance abuse in romantic relationships may look different when occurring in families. Unlike a romantic relationship where there are only two people involved, substance abuse in a family affects several people. Additionally, it can cause a dysfunctional dynamic between parents and children.

For example, in families suffering with addiction, it is common to find role reversal. The alcoholic parent may display neediness, throw tantrums, or deliberately start drama to seek attention—displaying tendencies that one would expect from a young child who lacks emotional intelligence. In contrast, the children may learn to be responsible from a young age and take on parental responsibilities, such as caring for younger siblings, advising how money should be spent, or showing greater emotional control than their parents.

Another interesting dynamic created in these types of families is the different roles each family member takes on in response to the dysfunctional home environment. Without being aware of it, each family member finds their own unique way of adjusting to the alcoholic parent's behaviors. You can think of this as their chosen way of coping in such a volatile family.

Earlier on, we spoke about the "golden child" who is the alcoholic's favorite child due to some level of giftedness they display. They learn to adapt to the unstable environment at home by focusing on things they can control, such as their participation in school sports or academic performance. The golden child begins to form an identity around their capabilities because that is the one area of life that seems stable and progressive and brings positive feedback.

The curse of the golden child is that they are forced to become the protégé of the alcoholic parent, a living example to the world that they are a responsible parent after all. The idea is that if they can raise a gifted child then they don't have such a serious drinking problem.

The golden child is typically shown a lot of affection by the alcoholic parent—more affection than anyone else in the home, including the codependent spouse. However, due to the alcoholic parent's self-centeredness, they only give their child affection when it serves them to do so. For instance, the parent might speak highly of the golden child in front of friends or when seeking to make other family members feel inadequate in comparison. But apart from those random moments, they show little interest in the child's well-being.

Some of the other family roles that may form in these types of families include the ones described here.

The Caretaker

The caretaker is the enabling spouse whose sense of purpose revolves around making the alcoholic partner's life comfortable. This often entails taking care of many of the household and financial responsibilities of the family, denying or downplaying the severity of their drinking problem, and keeping the family drama hidden from the outside world in order to protect the alcoholic's reputation. The caretaker's main priority is making sure their partner is happy, and at times, this means being emotionally unavailable for their children.

The Mascot

The mascot is the self-sacrificing child who feels it is their responsibility to make other family members feel good. They learn quite early in childhood how to modify their behaviors in order to relieve stress due to the alcoholic parent's behaviors. The relationship between the mascot and the alcoholic is superficial because the child learns to hide who they sincerely are and take on a light-hearted persona to uplift the atmosphere. They are typically seen as the clown of the family who always makes jokes and never takes things seriously. The truth however is that deep down the child has learned to suppress their needs in order to avoid conflict and make others happy.

The Lost Child

The lost child is usually the youngest sibling, who grows up feeling isolated from the rest of the family. They take on the role of observer rather than participant to all of the drama taking place at home. Other family members may think the lost child is the least affected by the dysfunctional environment because they are quiet and never express opposing views. In reality, the lost child has deep and complex feelings about what is happening but chooses to process things inside their head, in their own creative way. They may struggle with feelings of loneliness as an adult, which stem from spending a good portion of their childhood feeling distant from other family members.

The Scapegoat

The scapegoat is the outspoken child, normally the oldest, who has witnessed the bulk of the dysfunctional patterns at home. They have seen the negative impact of addiction on the family and feel resentment toward the alcoholic parent for perpetuating the chaos. They may also feel betrayed by the codependent parent for not doing enough to curb the substance abuse. The scapegoat may become rebellious as a form of protest against the authority of his or her parents. Their self-destructive behaviors give the alcoholic parent an excuse to divert the attention away from their drinking problem and onto the black sheep of the family.

Learning about the various relationship dynamics between a substance abuser and their partner or family members is important because it can explain how someone develops codependent behaviors. Looking at the dynamics above you might be able to think of someone, perhaps yourself, who has gone through similar experiences. You may have a history of dating, being married to, or being raised by someone who has an addiction, which has made it difficult to accept yourself, articulate your needs, or draw boundaries with others.

Perhaps you resonate with the golden child, who was praised for what they did instead of who they were, or the lost child, who craves but also fears expressing their needs and individuality in relationships. Take a few minutes to reflect on how substance abuse may have impacted your childhood and ability to form trusting and fulfilling relationships.

Emotional Abuse

Abuse can be defined as the improper use of a thing or improper treatment of a human being. The only way you can avoid mistreating an object or human being is to understand its purpose.

Think about the last time you purchased an electronic gadget or piece of furniture that needed to be fine-tuned or assembled. When you got home, you cut open the box, placed the individual components of the object on the table, and then what followed? That's right. You began to read the instruction manual. The reason for reading the manual was to understand the purpose of the object and how to operate it so that it could function according to the manufacturer's design.

It would have saved you time to skip the process of reading a lot of technical jargon and start assembling the gadget right away based on the knowledge you have about how it might function. But taking the shortcut would also increase the risk of building the gadget incorrectly and mishandling it.

What makes you fragile as a human being is the fact that you have a soul. Whenever you are placed in adverse situations, you react with stress and other strong emotions. It is a myth that males are less emotional than females or adults are more tolerant of pain than children. For as long as you are connected to your soul, regardless of your age, gender, or culture, your mind and body will react to being mistreated.

Parents bring little human beings into the world, but they aren't given an instruction manual on how to raise them properly and avoid mistreatment. This is what makes parenting the riskiest job that any individual could undertake. Even when it is not a parent's intention to mistreat their child, their oversight when it comes to protecting their child or being responsive to their needs can cause a lifetime of pain.

There are many types of abuse that a child can be exposed to, such as domestic, physical, and sexual abuse. These various circumstances can negatively affect their development and lead to codependency. In this section, we will zone in on one of the common types of abuse associated with codependency—emotional abuse.

We have touched on emotional abuse in previous chapters, mentioning emotional neglect and unresponsiveness as two ways that parents can be emotionally abusive to their children. What we haven't yet explored is the controlling and manipulative nature of emotional abuse.

Relationships that have a power imbalance, such as one person having more dominance over the other, are at risk of becoming emotionally abusive. This happens because the more powerful individual in the relationship can assert his or her own ideas about what is acceptable or unacceptable behavior, while the other individual feels obliged to go along with their agenda.

It is much easier to recognize and respond to a power imbalance in adult friendships or romantic relationships. However, the same cannot be said about parent-child relationships. The upper hand that parents have from the beginning is their position of authority. For the rest of their children's lives (even when they grow up and start their own families), the parents will always be in a position of authority.

There are parents who are mature enough to exercise this great amount of power with wisdom and self-restraint. Instead of doing what they want to do or saying whatever comes to mind, they consider the impact of their actions and words on the well-being of their children. They are also willing to share power with their older children by allowing them to express opposing views, decline to participate or follow through with a request, negotiate boundaries, and make decisions concerning their own lives. These types of parents usually build a secure attachment with their children and create a healthy foundation for future relationships.

Emotional abuse exists in parent-child relationships where there is a striking imbalance of power, and more than likely, parents have taken advantage of their position of power. In other words, they have misused their authority by intentionally or unintentionally exposing their children to harmful psychological experiences.

In cases where the misuse of authority is intentional, parents will create an environment that disempowers their children, causing them to feel a lack of control or hopelessness. The aim could be to make their children completely dependent on them to the extent of merging identities (i.e., becoming a "mini me"). Parents could also do it for other selfish reasons, like manipulating their children to cater to their needs.

Emotional abuse can cause children to develop codependent behaviors and feel helpless without their parents and, later in life, helpless without the validation of others. Even when children forge unstable and painful relationships with their parents, they feel sickly dependent on them and lost without them. This dependency occurs due to many years of being told what to do (and what not to do) and never being encouraged by their parents to trust their own gut instincts and make decisions that prioritize their own well-being.

There is a story often told about baby elephants who are trained to perform in a circus. While they are still weak and feeble, the animal instructors place chains around their legs and fasten the chains to strong pillars. Whenever the energetic young elephants attempt to escape, they feel a painful jerk on their legs. The pain creates a subconscious connection between running away and danger.

After months of being trained to be domesticated, the instructors remove the chains and allow the elephants to roam freely. At this stage of their development, they are considered adults due to the size of their bodies. However, since the elephants are still holding onto the memory of being chained to strong pillars and the pain of choosing to behave uncontrollably, they continue to behave as animals that are restrained.

This story sheds light on the after effects of suffering emotional abuse as a child, particularly how this experience can create codependent adults. The lack of respect, freedom of choice, and positive reinforcement shown by parents early in life can cause grown adults to seek after experiences or specific patterns of behavior that cause them to relive and repeat their childhood trauma.

They may not consciously want to hurt themselves (e.g., they do not deliberately chase after people who are bad for them), but being exposed to an unhealthy environment during those vulnerable childhood years creates a magnetic pull toward dysfunctional people and environments. In other words, not having their needs met as children has become so normalized by the time they are able to leave home that they feel comfortable entering adult relationships where their needs are not likely to be met.

Overprotective or Permissive Parenting

Unhealthy parenting styles can also lead to codependency later in life. We can define parenting styles as the attitudes and behaviors displayed by parents toward their children. Unlike attachments, which are based on a sacred bond between parents and children and often created unconsciously as a result of psychological issues, parenting styles are formed based on conscious habits that parents adopt when raising their children.

There are two particular parenting styles that are linked to codependency: overprotective and permissive parenting. If you consider each parenting style, you will notice that they describe attitudes and behaviors on opposite ends of the spectrum. For instance, overprotective parents tend to be controlling whereas permissive parents tend to be too laid back. Nevertheless, what these two parenting styles have in common is that in both instances, the parents are suffering from and responding to their own battles with codependency.

Overprotective parenting occurs when parents are hypersensitive to any possible danger that may befall their children, to the extent of making decisions on behalf of their children. The root of this behavior has nothing to do with protecting children from real or perceived threats in the environment but, rather, the parents' own fears of abandonment. It is about enforcing control over children to prevent them from potentially choosing to live their own lives. Thus, overprotective parents are likely to monitor their children's movements, create arbitrary rules to limit their children's freedoms, and display possessive tendencies.

It is common for overprotective parents to have trouble respecting their children's boundaries, which is due to their own lack of personal boundaries. Moreover, setting boundaries with their children might trigger their separation anxiety, a core fear that is rooted in their own childhoods. Due to the lack of boundaries, an overprotective parent doesn't see a real separation between them and their child. They may become emotionally dependent on their child to respond to their needs, provide a sense of safety and predictability, and constantly reassure them of their unconditional love and loyalty.

An example of overprotective parenting is a child (let's say a small boy) who is born into a dysfunctional family where his parent's marriage is toxic. His father may be an abuser who frequently mistreats his codependent mother. All of the red flags that indicate the marriage is loveless and dangerous are there, but the codependent mother stays regardless of the mistreatment because of her fear of being alone. Since her husband isn't providing the security and affection she deserves, she becomes overly dependent on her son to feed her emotional hunger.

As time goes on, she begins to fear life without her son. Perhaps she derives a sense of purpose from being a mother and cannot imagine the day that her son grows up and stops needing her. The bond with her son is symbolic of the love she has always yearned for, which she didn't receive as a young girl or in her marriage. So much is riding on this parent-child relationship that the mother starts tightening her grip on her son.

The danger of overprotective parenting is that it can lead to emotional incest, a psychological process where roles are reversed and the child is encouraged to act like an adult and respond to the parent's emotional needs. A typical example of emotional incest is when mothers treat their sons like their husbands, often making emotional demands that are inappropriate to ask of children.

For example, children cannot be expected to always empathize with their parents, spend hours talking on the phone with their parents, surprise their parents with special gifts, or always be complementary to their parents. These types of emotional demands are suitable to request in platonic or romantic adult relationships, not with children who are emotionally immature. Emotional incest is a form of abuse that can cause children to grow up too soon, have trouble expressing anger as adults, struggle to set boundaries or assert themselves with others, and feel emotionally bankrupt (which can affect their ability to express affection in adult relationships).

The second type of parenting style that leads to codependency is permissive parenting, which occurs when parents enforce minimal demands on their children. In these parent-child relationships, there are little to no rules, poor boundaries, and not enough structure to teach children the difference between acceptable and unacceptable behaviors. Permissive parents are also codependent but choose to display their dependency on their children differently.

For example, instead of being controlling, they will show love by stepping back and giving their children an abundance of freedom, hoping that by being permissive to every behavior, they can earn their children's love. It is possible that some permissive parents were raised to accept transactional love. They may have only received attention, affection, and acceptance by appealing to their parents' needs and interests. They grow up having the same expectations when parenting their children, believing that by being the "coolest" and "most chilled" parent ever, they can win over their children.

Children raised by permissive parents tend to grow up with an unstable sense of self and poor self-regulation and self-control. Facing the real world can be tough because society is built on systems, structure, and heavy consequences for bad behaviors. Since they grew up with little discipline and accountability, they are more susceptible to substance abuse, promiscuity, gambling problems, getting in trouble with the law, and other high-risk activities. Furthermore, they are likely to become codependent on others.

An example of permissive parenting is a child (let's say a small girl) who is raised by a hard-working single mother. The little girl never gets to see her mother very much because she is always at work; however, whenever she does spend those few odd moments with her mother, she is showered with gifts and affection. In their household, the young girl is given permission to act out any kinds of behaviors without being held accountable. In the past, nannies who have tried to discipline her were fired by her mother with immediate effect.

The young girl grows up with a sense of entitlement, poor emotional regulation, and a distorted sense of reality. After graduating from college, she feels unprepared to build a life of her own. Her mother continues to support her financially, which makes it hard for her to engage with real-life issues, develop emotional intelligence, or gain independence. Due to her insecurities and unpreparedness for life, she tends to lean on others for physical and emotional needs.

Parenting is not an easy job simply because there are a million ways to get it wrong and only a few ways to get it right. And since parents aren't given an instruction manual on how to raise each child, they may not always behave in ways that are in the best interests of their children. Developing self-awareness can help parents learn to see themselves as separate individuals from their children, who may have different thoughts, feelings, dreams, or fears.

Instead of raising their children based on what they would prefer, they can consider what would be desirable for their children. For example, rigid routines and arbitrary rules are not desirable for a child—regardless of their age, gender, or disabilities. While children need structure and support, they also benefit from being allowed to explore the world, make their own choices, and most importantly—being allowed to be a kid.

What overprotective and permissive parents may not fully accept is that they cannot force or manipulate their children into forming loving and long-lasting relationships. It is too much to expect children to fill an emotional void that began in childhood and requires therapy to heal. When children are used as a 24/7 emotional supply, they become wounded adults who are disconnected from their own emotions due to having to grow up too soon.

Chapter 4:

Early Signs of Identity Issues

One of the biggest surprises in this research was learning that fitting in and belonging are not the same thing. In fact, fitting in is one of the greatest barriers to belonging. –Brené Brown

How Being Raised in a Dysfunctional Family Affects Your Identity

Every child is born with an identity, but it takes secure and available parents to mirror the child's identity back to them. Unless parents mirror their child's identity, the child will grow up without a sense of awareness or being grounding in who they are.

Validating a child's physical and emotional experiences is one of the ways in which parents can help them discover who they are. For example, when a child performs desirable behavior, shows interest in a particular topic, or reveals a talent, offering positive reinforcement builds the child's competence. They might walk away feeling strong, smart, or kind, and gradually they can start to link certain positive traits and strengths with their identity.

Empathy is another strategy that parents use to help their child discover who they are. Empathy goes a step further than validating a child's experiences; it seeks to show acceptance for what they might be thinking or feeling regardless of whether the parent shares the same sentiments.

For example, when a child is upset, an empathetic parent will offer loving touch and sit in the moment with them. They may not understand what their child is upset about, but they give the child permission to express strong emotions.

After being shown empathy, the child might walk away feeling safe to explore a range of emotions in front of their parents without feeling judged. Furthermore, being curious about their emotions can help them feel safe exploring different aspects of their personality and even practicing techniques like self-soothing and emotional regulation.

One of the negative outcomes of being raised in a dysfunctional family is struggling to come to terms with who you are and where you fit into your family or the world at large. Due to the lack of stability and unconditional love at home, you may have learned to disconnect from your body. This is a common coping mechanism that children adopt to regulate themselves and reduce the likelihood of being re-traumatized.

If you were someone who grew up in a dysfunctional family, exploring your feelings or even spending time thinking about yourself didn't seem like something worth pursuing. Due to the ongoing tension or conflict around you, you didn't have the luxury to focus on developing your awareness. You may have felt uncomfortable in your own skin, perhaps wishing that you were somewhere else or somebody else.

The inability to grab or keep your parents' attention meant that you were unable to receive validation about who you are, and nobody could empathize with many of the challenges you were going through. The small bits of information you learned about yourself came from the beliefs, attitudes, and behaviors circulating in the house. This means that if your parents struggled with self-esteem issues, pessimistic thinking, or poor emotional regulation, you may have picked up on those behaviors and built a self-image out of them.

Being raised in a dysfunctional family didn't provide you with the goal-oriented assistance necessary in building a healthy identity. You probably had no other option but to learn about yourself from your interactions with peers at school or when you left home to attend college or start working.

Nevertheless, due to not being given a solid foundation to build your identity, many of the things you learned about yourself may not have been authentic (i.e., they may have been influenced by the people who were in your environment at the time).

Fortunately, this chapter of the book will take you back to the basics of identity formation, so you can build a solid foundation that informs who you are. You will also learn about the consequences of not having this solid foundation and how to prevent that from happening.

What Does It Mean to Have a Solid Sense of Self?

A sense of self, also known as a self-concept, is the ideas you hold about who you are. Depending on the information you are fed by your environment, you can develop a solid or weak sense of self.

Before babies start talking, they are already picking up cues about the nature of their environment, such as whether it is safe or not. Factors that can influence a baby's sense of safety include being in a stable and loving environment and how emotionally responsive their parents are.

Assuming that a baby is raised in a positive environment by emotionally responsive parents, they are able to develop trust with their parents, which makes it safe to explore the world and form connections with other people.

By the age of two and three, a toddler starts to develop a sense of self however basic it might be. For instance, they are able to show possession of things (e.g., "This is mine") and experience complex emotions like guilt or shame. At this age, they are also starting to notice the emotions of others, such as recognizing when their parents are upset.

When they reach preschool age, the child will show curiosity about their physical attributes and the physical attributes of others. During this time, they are starting to build a self-image and connecting their physical attributes to ideas and beliefs. For instance, they might formulate ideas about what it means to be a short or tall person, black or white person, or having a small or big nose.

Messages from their environment greatly influence how a preschooler describes and makes sense of their self-image. Positive messages that promote diversity and inclusion can increase their self-confidence and empathy toward others. In contrast, negative messages about their physical attributes can create insecurity (which could simply be interpreted as an uncomfortable feeling) about who they are.

It is only when the child reaches their adolescent years that they actively start seeking an identity. Before then, they may not have thought deeply about what makes them unique and where they fit in the world. However, the foundation for a healthy identity is set during those tender years, influenced by what the child experiences within their environment.

Three Critical Identity Developments

The probability of a teenager developing a solid sense of self is determined by the inputs from childhood. But since children are resilient, it is not too late for parents to intervene and play an active role in helping their teens form a healthy identity. There are three critical identity developments that must be made in order for a young person to grow up feeling comfortable in their own skin. Let's explore them now.

The Ability to Conceptualize Multiple Selves

An individual's self-concept is not set in stone. It is an idea they have about themselves which is constantly evolving. In order for teenagers to develop a strong sense of self they must be allowed—given the freedom—to explore who they could be. In a practical sense, this means that teens should be allowed to act out, test boundaries, make terrible choices, face the consequences of their actions, and repeat these processes until they discover who they want to be.

The refusal of parents to allow this kind of uninhibited behavior can result in a young person settling for "one type of self" which they don't resonate with but have to accept. This "one type of self" could be the only self the parents are willing to accept. Just imagine for a second that you were told who you should be and not given an option to discover for yourself who you actually are. How would you feel? How comfortable would you be expressing yourself?

The Ability to Differentiate From Others

Another critical identity development milestone is being able to differentiate "who I am and what I want" from "who you are and what you want." This step is important for building true confidence that is based on intrinsic worth rather than approval gained from others.

Differentiation occurs when a young person is capable of identifying and taking ownership of their thoughts and emotions while simultaneously rejecting taking ownership or merging with what others might think or feel. Second, differentiation requires the contextual understanding of why one might think or feel the way they do and the social or environmental factors that could be influencing their perceptions. Having this contextual understanding encourages empathy for others but also promotes individuality.

Most of the time, differentiation in teenagers can come across as rebellion against their parents. For example, the young person might refuse to take the advice of their parents because that isn't how they would respond to a particular situation. It takes emotionally intelligent parents to recognize that this behavior is a sign of independence, not disrespect, and resist the urge to use their authority to disempower their child.

The Ability to Develop High Self-Esteem

The third important step of identity development that needs to take place for young people to build a strong sense of self is developing high self-esteem. To esteem something is to hold it in high regard. Thus, adolescents with high self-esteem see themselves in a positive light.

It is expected that a young person's thoughts or feelings about themselves will change based on a number of environmental factors. For example, when they perform poorly at school, they might think negatively about themselves. But then an unexpected compliment might positively adjust their thoughts. Having high self-esteem allows for teens to manage the highs and lows of life without losing the unshakeable belief in themselves. They are able to experience loss or failure but quickly bounce back from the situation.

A young person with low self-esteem isn't capable of maintaining unshakable belief in themselves when they experience difficulties. They are more likely to crumble at the smallest setback or inconvenience. The thoughts and feelings they have about themselves are so discouraging that they aren't able to hold them up when challenges arise. In fact, their vulnerability to negative thoughts and emotions could cause them to avoid taking any action that might worsen how they already feel about themselves.

What helps young girls and boys build high self-esteem is different. For example, young girls develop high self-esteem from making and maintaining connections with their peers. The lack of socializing, emotional support, and acceptance into a peer group can lead to a low self-esteem.

In contrast, young boys develop high self-esteem from finding their voice, claiming their independence, and building favorable relationships with people in authority, such as parents, school teachers, and work bosses. Whenever young boys are denied opportunities to assert their beliefs, develop competence through learning skills, carve their own path, and gain influence at home or within the community, they may develop a low self-esteem.

Take the moment to reflect on your childhood and adolescence. Recall your earliest memories of discovering that you are a separate person with unique thoughts and feelings. Consider the three critical areas of identity development and how they may have featured in your life. For instance, what were some of the challenges you experienced conceptualizing multiple selves, undergoing the process of differentiation or developing high self-esteem? You are welcome to write down your thoughts and explore them at a later time.

The Consequences of Having an Unstable Sense of Self

It is important to emphasize that the opposite of a strong sense of self is not "no sense self." Every human being is born with a conscious mind, which means they have the capacity to think about themselves and their existence. However, this doesn't mean that what they think about themselves will always match reality.

The opposite of a strong sense of self then is an unstable sense of self. Simply put, an unstable sense of self refers to having distorted, complicated, or confusing ideas about who you are. According to psychoanalyst, Erik Erikson, individuals between the ages of 12 and 18 go through a stage of identity formation known as "identity versus confusion" (Lumen Learning, n.d.).

During this stage, one of two things can happen: They can either successfully answer the question "Who am I?" or they can develop an identity crisis, being confused about who they are. To avoid falling into a state of confusion, Teenagers must go through a process of questioning what they have been taught and coming up with their own ideas and conclusions. Borrowing from their parents' or peers' values and beliefs, they are encouraged to think about their own views. The result is not becoming a replica of their parents or friends but becoming their own person.

An unstable sense of self can lead to more complicated identity issues. For example, it could lead to an experience known as foreclosure, where a young person settles on a single identity without exploring their options. The second issue is known as identity confusion, where a young person decides to not identify as anything at all. They do not commit themselves to specific ideas, beliefs, or societal norms and roles about who they should be. The third issue is known as moratorium, where a young person continues to explore multiple selves without reaching the stage of settling on who they are.

Young people who choose an identity without exploring the "possible selves" tend to make a single identifier the center of who they are. For example, they might build an identity around their religion, politics, culture, competence, or gender. This decision could be based on receiving pressure from their parents to align beliefs and follow the traditions of the family, or it could be self-imposed pressure to skip the journey of self-discovery and quickly settle on something.

In adulthood, an unstable sense of self can lead to codependent behaviors, such as adjusting your personality depending on who you are speaking to and being agreeable to avoid being challenged and asserting your own beliefs. It can also make individuals more prone to staying in unhealthy friendships, work relationships, or romantic relationships due to the fear of being alone.

Codependency causes individuals to build a sense of self around an important relationship. If there are no boundaries within the relationship to prevent enmeshment, the codependent individual can find themselves being lost in the other person's world and developing new personality traits, interests, and goals based on what the other person enjoys and desires.

As much as codependent people crave connection, it can be helpful for them to take some time to figure out who they are and what they want out of life before jumping from one failed relationship to another. Having a strong sense of self is what makes healthy relationships feel so incredibly fulfilling.

Picture in your mind: Two individuals with different life stories and personalities come together to exchange ideas, learn from each other, and broaden their understanding of life, love, and purpose. Doesn't that sound better than two halves that depend on each other to feel whole?

Chapter 5:

Going Beyond People-Pleasing

When you say yes to others make sure you are not saying no to yourself. —Paulo Coelho

How Codependency Affects Your Self-Worth

When asked to describe codependency, most people would start talking about people-pleasing. Yes, it's true. People-pleasing, which refers to sacrificing your own wants and needs to appeal to the interests of others, is a behavioral symptom of codependency. However, this is only the tip of the iceberg.

At the core of codependency are a host of identity issues that emerge during childhood as a result of not receiving the security and validation you needed from your parents. Over time, the inability to come to terms with and embrace who you are causes you to feel unworthy.

The feeling of being unworthy is triggered by low self-esteem as well as being exposed to abuse or neglect in your environment. For instance, if you had a critical parent who constantly put you down, their piercing words may have tainted the perception you hold about yourself. Even if, at first, you didn't believe what they were saying about you, on a subconscious level, your own self-beliefs and attitudes were being influenced by their harsh words.

Codependency develops out of a need to be needed. The reason you may have a compulsive need to be of use to others could be because you are seeking to affirm that you are worthy. Perhaps the only way you can feel worthy internally is to be productive and add value to other people's lives externally.

This explains why altruism and codependency often get confused with each other. Both individuals seek to be of value to others, but what drives them to do so is different. Don't get me wrong, being codependent doesn't mean you are conceited in doing good for others; however, extending yourself to others offers a heart-warming validation that someone who is altruistic isn't searching for.

Codependent people can display both altruistic and people-pleasing tendencies. The difference between altruism and people-pleasing is that one behavior empowers while the other disempowers. If you choose to go the altruistic route, you go out of your way to help others for the sake of making a difference in the world.

Generously giving up your time, money, and skills makes you feel proud, responsible, and socially conscious. People-pleasing, on the other hand, involves a personal sacrifice, deliberately pushing aside your ideas, interests, and feelings to accommodate other people. There is no personal satisfaction gained from people-pleasing. You don't feel proud of yourself or derive any pleasure from your generous giving.

The purpose of this chapter is to look beyond people-pleasing and explore the consequences of not feeling worthy, particularly in relationships. The focus will be on discussing behaviors that signal low self-worth to help you understand the costs of sacrificing your needs in efforts to make other people happy. While having a selfless attitude is a wonderful virtue, it is important to be aware of your personal limits and know when to step back, draw healthy boundaries, and prioritize your own well-being.

Weak or Rigid Boundaries

One of the consequences of low self-worth that you may or may not experience is boundary issues. You might have weak, nonexistent boundaries, rigid and cutthroat boundaries, or switch between the two.

Not every codependent person wears their heart on their sleeve and jumps head first into relationships. There are some who are closed off and deliberately make it hard for others to get to know them. The result is that their boundaries are either extremely weak or rigid.

You may be wondering what these boundaries look like in real-life situations. First, let us define and explore weak boundaries. A weak boundary is a rule or limitation that isn't strengthened by a clear purpose and consequences to hold others accountable. As such, it becomes difficult to enforce a weak boundary because it isn't backed by a strong conviction.

Some weak boundaries are so unclear or confusing (i.e., exhibiting contradictory behavior) that people don't take them seriously. For example, if you tell a colleague that you are unavailable to chat over the weekend but continue to respond to their texts or emails, they will eventually step over the boundary.

If you tend to create weak boundaries, it is possible that you grew up without being given permission to assert your needs. Most of the decisions made during childhood or adolescence were chosen by your parents. Thus, even as an adult, you tend to "go with the flow" and respond to other people's behaviors rather than setting expectations.

It is important to emphasize that having weak boundaries doesn't make you weak. It simply means that you don't have a strong enough conviction to back your wishes. In other words, you are extremely flexible and accommodating of others, which sometimes can inconvenience you.

Below are some examples of weak boundaries in relationships:

- You agree to plans that you internally disagree with.

- You overextend yourself to the point of exhaustion.

- You overbook yourself to avoid letting other people down.

- You don't speak up when others mistreat you.

- You fear being criticized for sharing your thoughts or feelings.

- You accept blame for things that you know you didn't do.

- You take on responsibilities that are not yours.

It is also common to switch from setting weak to rigid boundaries. This typically happens during the early stages of breaking free from codependency, when you are still learning what healthy limits look like. In efforts to assert yourself and protect your interests, you can go overboard and set boundaries that are too rigid.

A rigid boundary can be defined as a limit that is impenetrable and unadjustable. It doesn't take into consideration the highs and lows of life, how people may have bad days, or how plans can sometimes change. You may see the world as black-and-white, treat people as good or bad, and respond to situations without empathy.

Another sign of a rigid boundary is being detached from other people's experiences. For instance, a boss with rigid boundaries has cutthroat rules that don't consider employees' personal lives or emergency crises that may occur from time to time. When their strict boundaries are violated, they resort to harsh disciplinary actions without seeking to understand where the other person is coming from.

There is no denying that rigid boundaries offer more safety than weak boundaries. However, the drawback is that they can be very isolating. When your boundaries are too fixed, you may unconsciously start pushing people away. Small offenses may result in big consequences, like cutting friends off, ending romantic relationships, and ultimately sabotaging healthy connections.

Some of the signs of rigid boundaries in relationships include

- being intolerant of loved ones making mistakes or having bad days
- distancing yourself from people who have offended you, without observing patterns or talking about your problem
- expecting more than an apology after someone has offended you
- being inflexible when faced with unique circumstances or arrangements
- refusing to see where other people are coming from

- being highly sensitive to criticism and rejection; seeing people who disagree with you as "bad" and those who agree with you as "good"

The switch between weak and rigid boundaries could also be triggered by perceived rejection or abandonment. For example, at the beginning of a relationship, you may overshare, selflessly give your all, and completely open up to your partner. But as soon as you pick up on subtle changes in your dynamic, such as your partner being busy or taking longer to text back, you may switch to rigid boundaries.

Now all of a sudden, you are emotionally withdrawn, strict about when and how much you meet up, start unnecessary fights, or make them pay each time they trigger your emotional wounds. This cycle of push and pull is rooted in a fear of intimacy or vulnerability—stemming from your fear of rejection or abandonment. The longer the cycle continues, the more toxic and unsalvageable the relationship will be.

Later in the book, you will learn how to go from setting weak or rigid boundaries to setting healthy, relationship-building boundaries!

Comparing Yourself to Others

Having low self-worth causes you to see the value in others but seldomly find the value within yourself. This means that you tend to judge others based on their positive attributes, then turn around and judge yourself based on your worst attributes.

Warren Buffett put it this way: "The big question about how people behave is whether they've got an inner scorecard or an outer scorecard. It helps if you can be satisfied with an inner scorecard" (Farnam Street, 2019, para.2).

One of the behaviors that can trigger your personal feelings of inadequacy is comparing yourself to other people. You might rank your attractiveness, competence, or success based on where your peers are, what they have, or the current status quo in society. What makes this behavior self-destructive is that you give people and external circumstances the power to determine your self-worth.

For example, you may only feel good about yourself when you are validated or recognized by others. Knowing that you are on par or doing better than your peers may give you a sense of power and control. This is especially true when you have built an identity around your competence. The danger with comparing yourself to others is that it creates an unending cycle of wanting to prove yourself. It doesn't matter how brilliant you were in the past, your goal is to constantly be the best.

At first, this goal may keep you motivated to work harder. But, with time, it can lead to a host of insecurities stemming from not feeling good enough. In relationships, comparing yourself to your friends, colleagues, or romantic partners can breed jealousy, unhealthy competition, manipulation, and other narcissistic tendencies. Instead of celebrating other people's differences, you might perceive them as threats.

An example of this is a man who at first delights in his lady's intelligence but, after a while, begins to resent it because it makes him feel insecure. The issue isn't that she is smart but that in comparison to her, the man doesn't feel smart enough. He might respond to his insecurities by picking up a course, learning a new skill, and going to extremes to make himself feel on par or above his lady's level of intelligence. Alternatively, he might put her down and act unkind in order to make himself feel better.

Notice how whenever you feel the need to compare yourself to others, you begin to lose control of your thoughts, emotions, and behaviors. You may even get sidetracked from following your own goals and adopt new behaviors and interests that do not match your ideal lifestyle. Ending the cycle of making comparisons starts with accepting yourself for who you are—flaws and all. Acceptance and self-compassion are necessary to avoid turning against yourself and becoming your own worst enemy.

Later in the book, you will be taught how to transform the relationship you have with yourself and accept the "ugly parts" you struggle to accept through practicing alternative therapies like inner child healing and shadow work.

The Need for Excessive Control

It is normal to want to feel in control of your life. Self-control is one of the best ways to build self-discipline and live a stable and structured lifestyle. However, excessive need for control isn't about creating stability, it is about having power.

There is a clear difference between healthy control and excessive control. Healthy control is about improving the way you manage your life, such as developing positive habits by making better choices. The goal is to create a harmonious life while steadily improving the way you live.

Excessive control has very little to do with enhancing the way you live. Instead it is about having power over external factors, such as people or outcomes. This need for power stems from feeling disempowered in past experiences—think of it as a way of making up for past injustices.

There are a multitude of reasons why you may have felt disempowered in the past, ranging from personal limitations to the environment you were raised in. Whether the message was implied or said explicitly, you didn't believe you were worthy of positive experiences. In reverse, this meant believing that nothing good could happen to you unless it was self-directed; the only way to make good things happen was to take matters into your own hands and literally make things happen.

To make an illustration, picture a young girl who grows up diagnosed with autism and has trouble building and maintaining friendships throughout her adolescence. On a psychological level, the lack of connection leaves her feeling rejected and disempowered. She enters her 20s feeling lonely and desperate for community—the perfect recipe for codependent relationship patterns.

However, since she unconsciously believes she doesn't deserve genuine friendships, she struggles to allow new relationships to naturally blossom at their own pace and time. She feels the need to make her relationships work by being overly controlling of her friends and doing more than she needs to keep the friendships going.

The excessive need for control is a form of self-sabotage. It leads to crossing boundaries, perfectionist thinking, anxiety about relationships, and finding it difficult to accept people or outcomes for who and what they are. This type of behavior can also attract abusers and manipulators (at work and socially) who take advantage of your willingness to always help, fix problems, and offer ongoing support.

In the chapter, you will learn one particularly useful intervention that can help you manage the excessive need to control others—loving detachment.

Exercises to Rebuild Self-Worth

Having read through three of the many consequences of low self-worth, you may be interested to learn different ways to build and enhance your self-worth. A healthy and stable self-worth is built on having a clear and unshakeable understanding of who you are. Just think about it: When you understand who you are, you are capable of setting and communicating healthy limits with others, you don't feel the need to compare yourself to others, and you don't have a burning desire to control external factors because you are secure within yourself.

Self-understanding includes thinking about every small element that makes you who you are, including those quirky behaviors that others may not accept or grapple with. Self-understanding is also about understanding what you are capable of, where your weaknesses lie, and some of the past issues you are still working through so you can make a fair and balanced assessment of your life without leaning too much toward the positive or negative extremes.

There is so much about your life that you haven't uncovered or looked at long enough to understand. These question marks create room for confusion, outside influence, or fears to take hold of you. Self-understanding brings enlightenment, which helps you connect with the truth about who you are; you slowly start learning how to see every aspect of yourself, the good and ugly, rather than zooming in on a single aspect of who you are.

This process can be both eye-opening and uncomfortable because it enables you to see the person behind your age, gender, net worth, occupation, social status, or relationship status. You get the opportunity to be acquainted with the real you, not your "best self" or your "worst self."

A useful technique to practice when rebuilding your self-worth is journaling. This technique makes it easier to keep track of your insights and draw patterns from spontaneous thoughts. Simple journal prompts can spark many pages of reflections about who you are.

Prompts are also open-ended enough to allow for greater curiosity and self-awareness.

There are three journal-based exercises that can begin the process of rebuilding your self-worth. Grab a pen and notebook and answer the following prompts to the best of your ability (at your own time and pace).

Journal Exercise 1: How Well Do You Understand Yourself?

The first exercise assesses how well you know yourself, beyond the superficial facts about your life. You will be challenged to reflect on your thoughts and feelings about life, specifically thoughts and feelings that are unique to you!

Answer the following prompts to get to know yourself better:

- If everything you owned, worked hard for, and brought you happiness (e.g., possessions, achievements, friends and family) were taken away from you, what would remain? What value cannot be taken away?

- What personal quality makes you memorable, different from others? Describe this quality and scenarios where it shows up.

- What experience from the past do you still struggle to get over or make peace with?

- How do other people see you? Reflect on how you present yourself to the world. Note that this self-image could be different from who you actually are, and that is okay.

- Write about three core memories that define who you are. These can be pleasant or unpleasant memories from childhood, adolescence, or adulthood. Moreover, they could be memories involving other people or moments spent by yourself.

- What recurring fears hold you back from fully stepping into your greatness. Write down your fears and explore where they come from and how they have impacted your life.

- Which areas of your life do you consistently let yourself down? Describe the various ways you may inflict pain on yourself, knowingly or unknowingly. What tends to trigger these behaviors?

- Complete this sentence: Given the choice, I would not trade my life for anybody else's because…

Now that you have a better understanding of who you are, let's proceed to the next exercise about self-acceptance.

Journal Exercise 2: How Much Do You Accept Yourself?

The next exercise explores the subject of self-acceptance. Rebuilding your self-worth is about being at peace with who you are. The reason why this is often easier said than done is because there could be a multitude of things you don't like about yourself. If you asked any random person on the street to rate how comfortable they feel in their own body, very few people would score themselves a 10/10.

Perhaps if there wasn't so much pressure in society to conform to rigid standards of beauty, success, and health, it wouldn't be so hard to actually reach a stage of being content with your life. However, in every direction you turn, you are always reminded of what you don't have and how your life could be so much better.

You may find journaling about self-acceptance tougher than journaling about who you are. Many of us are able to identify what makes us unique, but that doesn't mean we accept those qualities about ourselves. To make the journaling process more enjoyable, your task is to write letters to your younger self. Each letter should be based on a different theme, which you can explore in your own way, to whatever depth you are comfortable with. These letters will not be shared with anybody else, so you are free to be as open and honest as possible.

Here are the themes for each letter:

- loss, failure, and disappointment

- forgiveness, letting go, reconciliation

- character flaws, developmental challenges, and weaknesses

There are no rules about how long or detailed your letters should be or how much of the theme you are able to cover. If you really enjoy the exercise, you can give yourself a challenge to cover subtopics from each theme every month! Make this journaling process your own so you can get the most out of it.

Journal Exercise 3: How Much Do You Love Yourself?

The concept of self-love can be cringe to think about, especially when you don't have a history of being affirmed in your relationships. As a recovering codependent person, you may be accustomed to think about others or find things that are praiseworthy about others, putting yourself last. However, to truly love and accept others, you must first develop a genuine love and acceptance for yourself.

Have you ever heard the phrase, "You cannot pour from an empty cup"? What it means is that you cannot offer others what you don't offer yourself. It isn't too difficult to imagine how this plays out in the real world. Think about the times when you felt the most insecure about yourself and how you showed up in relationships. Would you have described yourself as a loving and understanding person back then? Perhaps not. Harboring insecurities could have made you deeply self-conscious and judgmental of yourself, which spilled over to how you related with others.

Now think of the first time you had an "Aha!" moment (a moment of clarity or revelation). Maybe you overcame a fear, finally let go of holding on to past pain, or discovered a positive quality about yourself. How did the "Aha!" moment transform the relationship you had with yourself and, subsequently, the relationships you had formed with others? Were you more relaxed, social, and accepting of others afterward? If so, the change of attitude toward your relationships had something to do with the change of attitude toward yourself.

Circling back to the topic of self-love, the degree to which you show concern and compassion to others can be influenced by the degree to which you show concern and compassion to yourself. Before you can sincerely answer the question, "How much do you love your parents, spouse, or children?," you must first contend with the bigger question, "How much do you love yourself?"

As a codependent person, you are accustomed to extending yourself to others, but is that behavior born out of habit or genuine devotion? In other words, are you simply self-sacrificing because that is how you were brought up to relate to others, or have you reached the stage where you give from a place of abundance? Self-love is cultivated from a place of abundance—an abundance of inner joy, peace, and gratitude. Being at peace with yourself allows you to maintain an internal environment that is kind, gentle, and nurturing despite the challenges you may be faced with in the external world.

To explore the subject of self-love more deeply, reflect upon and answer the following journal prompts:

- Your definition of love evolves as you gain more experience. Identify and write about three milestone events that caused you to look at love differently.

- The relationship you have with yourself is often the most complicated relationship in your life. Describe the highs and lows of your own love story. Remind yourself of the disconnect and tumultuous relationship you have had with yourself over time as well as some of the breakthroughs and opportunities for self-forgiveness and healing you have experienced.

- Self-love is not about always feeling positive; instead, it is a commitment to taking care of yourself no matter the circumstances. Think of a few examples of times when you have fully shown commitment to taking care of yourself and the actions you took that made you feel safe and supported.

- One of the barriers to self-love is the false and harmful beliefs you learned about yourself. These beliefs make it hard relating to yourself in a compassionate way. Identify what some of these beliefs are and provide conclusive evidence that they are not true. Provide a compelling case against them, which can help you break free from those discouraging thoughts.

- There were times in the past when you were a difficult person to love. You may have behaved in ways that were disappointing and didn't reflect the authentic version of you. Nevertheless, you stuck it out and made it through that difficult period. If you had an opportunity to thank your younger self for never giving up on your potential, what specific things would you thank them for?

Rebuilding your self-worth takes more than three amazing exercises. It is important to see this process as a lifetime journey rather than a crash course. These journal exercises are meant to introduce you to the multifaceted journey of rebuilding your self-worth. They will crack the surface and get you thinking about important themes in your life.

To truly maximize your effectiveness in rebuilding your self-worth—and combat boundary issues, identity issues, control issues, and, most importantly, codependency issues—there are plenty of additional interventions that will be shared in the following chapters!

Chapter 6:

Breaking the Cycle of Codependency

Detachment is based on the premise that each person is responsible for himself, that we can't solve problems that aren't ours to solve, and that worrying doesn't help. –Melody Beattie

What Are the Stages of Codependency?

The goal for this book is to help you break free from codependency. However, in order to achieve this aim, you must be able to recognize patterns of codependency within yourself. It is worth mentioning again that codependency has different faces—not everyone will display the same symptoms or the same level of intensity. Therefore, your task in breaking free from codependency is to understand which stage you are currently at and the unique way codependency manifests in your life.

An easy way to understand codependency is to think of it as a behavioral condition that manifolds as stages. Each stage leads to the next until you reach the most critical stage where you need to seek professional help from therapists to get a hold of your codependency issues. Below is a breakdown of each stage and a variety of symptoms you may experience (it is also possible that you don't experience all of the symptoms mentioned below).

Early Stage

The early stage of codependency can be difficult to identify because the behaviors you exhibit seem normal. For example, if a colleague asks for a favor, wouldn't you agree to help them out? Or if a loved one was going through a tough time, wouldn't you rush to their side and seek to alleviate their suffering?

To some extent, every human being who has ever cared for someone falls under this stage of codependency. Signs of being kind and considerate of others, such as paying attention to them, responding to their needs, or having the desire to please them (this can also manifest in work relationships) can also double as early signs of codependency.

The determining factor of whether these innocent displays of affection could potentially become unhealthy is when you find yourself rationalizing another person's mistreatment instead of holding them accountable, thinking obsessively about them, and being afraid or unable to set healthy boundaries (i.e., your boundaries are either weak or rigid).

Middle Stage

Learning to assert yourself and set boundaries in relationships can save you from graduating to the middle stage of codependency. Almost everyone who enters this stage cannot say no to a specific person or people they hold dear. Besides experiencing boundary issues, your fear of abandonment may be triggered by the proximity you have with someone, which causes you to feel anxious, insecure, and overwhelmed by the relationship.

Instead of enjoying the experience of getting to know someone, you may find yourself becoming preoccupied with making sure they enjoy your company, reciprocate your feelings, and feel as strong of a connection to you as you feel toward them. These anxious thoughts can cause you to start compromising your likes and dislikes, emotional well-being, and interests and hobbies. The dark side to this is that you could also look for ways to control the other person into needing you through guilt-tripping, creating dependency (e.g., making them rely on you financially), or manipulation.

It is not too late to turn back when you discover that you have reached the middle stage. However, it takes a great deal of courage to challenge your negative thoughts, control your urges, and respect your own boundaries and those of the other person. Whenever your abandonment wound is triggered, you can see it as an opportunity to practice self-care and spend time nursing your own feelings.

Late Stage

When you reach the late stage of codependency, your fears have become so unrestrained that your mental and emotional well-being start to suffer. At their lowest, your relationships may look and feel similar to the unhealthy attachment you had with your parents. The same behavioral patterns are reenacted, which trigger you to resort to the same coping strategies you used as a child, such as becoming passive, emotionally checking out, and being afraid to speak up for yourself.

Seeking help from an external party is important at this stage. It gives you an opportunity to see your relationship patterns through the eyes of an unbiased outsider, whose only desire is to help you regain control over your life. Another reason why you may need third-party support is due to experiencing co-occurring stress-related disorders that require a medical diagnosis, such as generalized anxiety disorder, obsessive-compulsive disorder, depression, insomnia, substance abuse problems, or an eating disorder.

What is important to emphasize is that at any stage, there are processes you can follow to break free from codependency. You may not show severe signs of the condition, but that doesn't mean you cannot benefit from taking preventative measures. Even healthy relationships that don't show any signs of codependency can benefit from practicing interventions to prevent the condition from occurring.

Interventions to Break the Cycle of Codependency

It is common for codependent people to feel a sense of shame or failure when they think about the state of their relationships, such as being upset with themselves for being overly invested in the well-being of others or not receiving the validation or closeness they are looking for. This sense of shame can make them feel embarrassed for seeking help.

Codependency is not a sign of weakness or failure. It is simply an unhealthy approach to showing affection for others. The fact that you are a fierce and passionate person, who goes all-in when they care about people is something to be proud of, something that makes you unique. Nevertheless, to avoid exhausting yourself or triggering past emotional wounds, you will need to learn how to love others in healthier ways. Below are three interventions that can help you prevent or manage codependent tendencies in relationships.

Cognitive Behavioral Therapy

Cognitive behavioral therapy (CBT) is a type of psychotherapy that is structured around identifying, describing, and adjusting unwanted emotions, thoughts, and behaviors. The goal of CBT is to help you make sense of difficult psychological experiences and find positive ways to respond, without hurting yourself or others.

For example, when you start overthinking, what do you normally do? Based on your answer, is that particular action or behavior helpful in restoring mental clarity and calmness? CBT encourages you to question, challenge, and confront those troublesome emotions or thoughts that you often push down, downplay, or get triggered by.

Practicing CBT, whether it is through formal therapy sessions with a licensed CBT practitioner or carrying out exercises at home, can help you manage symptoms of codependency like obsessive thinking, acting on impulses, creating weak or rigid boundaries, and other unproductive behaviors. Typical CBT exercises can help you respond to codependency triggers in the following positive ways:

- Challenge negative thinking patterns by sticking to the facts and looking for evidence to justify thoughts.

- Acknowledge and describe a range of emotions to better understand what you may be feeling and find appropriate ways to calm yourself.

- Observe frantic and anxiety-provoking thoughts without self-identifying with them or acting upon them.

- Create a prevention plan to manage emotional triggers, fight destructive urges, and manage stress in relationships.

- Learn the difference between helpful and harmful behaviors by assessing the impact of your actions to your well-being and the quality of your relationships.

Note that CBT doesn't heal codependency as such. Rather, it addresses the thoughts, emotions, and behaviors that make you vulnerable to developing codependency. The same therapy is effective in treating co-occurring disorders like chronic stress, anxiety, depression, and obsessions.

What makes CBT effective is its ability to make you think about unconscious thoughts and feelings you wouldn't normally think about. Doing this gives you an opportunity to choose helpful thoughts, emotions, and behaviors. The power of choice is what helps you break free from codependency!

Codependents Anonymous

Codependents Anonymous (CoDA) is a support group for men and women who desire to break free from codependency. Similar to the Alcoholics Anonymous (AA) program, they host online and physical meetings where visitors and members gather to discuss their struggles and victories in developing healthy relationships. Anybody can apply to become a member; the only requirement is that they display a willingness to heal from codependency and build positive relationships.

Another similarity to the AA program is its reliance on 12 steps and traditions to gain wisdom, hold each other accountable, and begin the process of healing. Both the 12 steps and traditions are the same as those used in the AA program, except where the AA program would refer to alcohol or alcohol abuse, CoDA refers to codependency. What makes it different from AA, however, are the 12 promises that every member is encouraged to keep. The 12 promises are outlined below (Codependents Anonymous, n.d.):

1. I know a new sense of belonging. The feeling of emptiness and loneliness will disappear.

2. I am no longer controlled by my fears. I overcome my fears and act with courage, integrity and dignity.

3. I know a new freedom.

4. I release myself from worry, guilt, and regret about my past and present. I am aware enough not to repeat it.

5. I know a new love and acceptance of myself and others. I feel genuinely lovable, loving and loved.

6. I learn to see myself as equal to others. My new and renewed relationships are all with equal partners.

7. I am capable of developing and maintaining healthy and loving relationships. The need to control and manipulate others will disappear as I learn to trust those who are trustworthy.

8. I learn that it is possible to mend—to become more loving, intimate and supportive. I have the choice of communicating with my family in a way which is safe for me and respectful of them.

9. I acknowledge that I am a unique and precious creation.

10. I no longer need to rely solely on others to provide my sense of worth.

11. I trust the guidance I receive from my Higher Power and come to believe in my own capabilities.

12. I gradually experience serenity, strength, and spiritual growth in my daily life."

CoDA extends support to new members by offering them a Sponsor, a recovering member who has been in the program for a while, who takes the role of a mentor and guides the Sponsee (new member) through the 12 steps. However, since this support group is focused on healing codependency, there are specific rules of engagement that both Sponsor and Sponsee must follow to maintain a healthy and supportive relationship. Some of the rules include having a plan for regular meetings and what questions will be discussed on the call, limiting the call to only 15 minutes, and accepting that the Sponsor or Sponsee can end the relationship at any time with a verbal or written notice. Both Sponsors and Sponsees are also given goals that each of them are accountable to.

Loving Detachment

A common root cause of codependency are attachment wounds from childhood. For some reason or another, the relationship with one or both of your parents created a giver and taker dynamic. As the codependent child, you gave everything you could to be the ideal son or daughter, make your parents proud, and absorb as much of their pain as you humanly could.

However, the giver and taker dynamic didn't stop when you enter adulthood; the pattern continued to play out in specific adult relationships (remember that it is possible to display codependency in one relationship and not another). Whenever this dynamic shows up in an adult relationship, it causes you to become overly concerned or invested in another person's well-being.

An uncomfortable but effective intervention to disrupt the giver and taker dynamic and prevent you from crossing boundaries is called loving detachment. At face value, loving detachment sounds very cold. Why on earth would someone want to detach from the one they love? Wouldn't that trigger their abandonment wound?

It is only when you get to explore what loving detachment means and the freedom it provides that you can truly appreciate this exercise. According to the

Hazelden Betty Ford Foundation, loving detachment can be defined as caring enough about someone to allow them to make choices and learn from their mistakes (Martin, 2020). It is about respecting another person's humanity and individuality enough to not impose yourself into their life or take on their responsibilities.

There are a few things that loving detachment is not. Let's explore these differences.

Loving Detachment Is Not The Same as Cutting People Out of Your Life

Unless the person whom you have become sickly dependent on is abusive, there is no need to cut ties with them when you practice loving detachment. Detachment is not the same as turning your back on those you love but, instead, taking a step back from being overly invested and entangled in their lives.

In other words, you create enough room for both of you to have a life outside of each other, which means focusing on your own routines, setting personal goals, expanding your social circle to include other people, and so on. Of course, you will still make time each day, week, or month (depending on the nature of your relationship) to reconnect and deepen your bond. However, your worlds do not revolve around each other.

Loving Detachment Is Not Becoming Aloof and Creating a Wall Between You and Others

Once again, unless the person you have become dependent on is toxic, there is no need to put up your guard and create rigid boundaries with them. Remember that aside from the extreme attachment to one another, your relationship is actually quite beautiful!

There is no need to shut the other person out, create arbitrary rules, or practice no contact. Loving detachment is simply about creating space for them to be their own person, while you continue to be your own person. It encourages a shift from codependency to interdependence, whereby you still need each other but not in a stressful and overwhelming way.

Loving Detachment Is Not the Same as Cutting Back From Giving or Showing Support to Loved Ones

It is important for those who are on their codependency recovery journey to be careful not to take extreme decisions in an effort to correct their codependent patterns. The aim of recovery is to cultivate healthy relationships that are safe and balanced.

With that being said, loving detachment does not encourage withholding love, support, or generosity from others. Not only will this type of behavior promote impulsivity and distorted thinking, but it can also unfairly turn you into somebody you are not.

For instance, if you find joy in encouraging people, you shouldn't need to change that aspect of your identity while healing from codependency. Of course, how you show up for others will need to be adjusted through clear boundaries (examples of this will be given later in the book); however, you can still express affection in your unique love language.

Loving detachment is about accepting factors outside of your control rather than trying desperately to fix or change them. Since you cannot change another human being, you learn to accept them for who they are and how they choose to show up at each moment. This means that you respond to their words and actions at face value instead of assuming they meant something else. It also means holding others accountable for their actions by enforcing the proper consequences.

What makes loving detachment empowering throughout your codependency recovery is that it can help you set standards for how others treat you without focusing on how your standards make them feel. For example, if you set a boundary with your significant other to not raise their voice while speaking to you, it becomes easier to hold them accountable when they violate the boundary.

Practicing loving detachment would mean excusing yourself from the conversation without feeling guilty. You don't walk away because you have rejected your partner or seek to punish them for their poor choice of behavior. Instead you walk away because you accept the choice they made in that moment (i.e., choosing to cross a boundary) and you are willing to step back and allow them to face the consequences (i.e., not being allowed to continue engaging with you further).

If you are interested in practicing loving detachment in your relationships, practice the Five steps of detachment outlined below.

Acknowledge How You Might Be Feeling

Before deciding to lovingly detach or not, redirect your focus on how you are feeling. In the heat of the moment, you may be so consumed about how the other person behaved that you forget to check-in about how you feel. Acknowledging how you feel is an act of self-love, a way to comfort yourself after being disturbed by an experience. Give yourself a few days to process how you are feeling if you need to.

Practice Self-Inquiry

The second step is still about you! Once you have acknowledged your feelings, take the time to reflect on the story behind them. In other words, why did the situation trigger those specific emotions? Where and when did the story begin? What happened then that you are still processing now? The process of self-inquiry can be done through meditation, journaling, or any other exercise that encourages you to self-reflect.

Take Creative Action

When you have fully processed your feelings and understood where the boundary was crossed or why you felt offended, taken for granted, or mistreated, it is time to lovingly detach. Note that you won't always instinctively know how to lovingly detach, such as what actions to take. This is why it is useful to think creatively about the different ways you can approach the situation. For example, some situations might call for firmer boundaries, while others might call for a tough conversation followed by natural consequences (e.g., letting them suffer the natural outcomes of behaving a certain way). After brainstorming a few possible approaches, sleep on it, and only make the decision when you are certain that it is the best choice for you!

Find the Positive Lesson

There is something to be gained by both parties when you are lovingly detaching from others. Some of the advantages for you include building self-respect, strengthening your independence, resisting the urge to seek external validation, and practicing advocating for your needs. The other person can also benefit from your loving detachment. For example, they get to learn how to solve their own problems, confront unhealthy habits that are getting in the way of your relationship, and get to know you for who you are—not who they desire you to be. Give yourself time after taking creative action to reflect on the lessons you are walking away with.

Embrace Your Freedom

The final step is what makes loving detachment worth practicing! After you have ceased to control the situation, fix another person, or take responsibility for something you didn't cause, you get the chance to inhale freedom and exhale the stress and anxiety you may have been holding in. Remind yourself that practicing loving detachment is not a form of punishment but a ticket out of a toxic and unending codependent cycle. Each time you successfully reach this stage, find a small way to reward yourself.

In later chapters, we will be referring a lot to loving detachment when discussing healthy boundaries and strategies on how to address codependency issues in friendships, romantic relationships, and work relationships.

Chapter 7:
Healing Begins With Acceptance

Because one believes in oneself, one doesn't try to convince others. Because one is content with oneself, one doesn't need others' approval. Because one accepts oneself, the whole world accepts him or her. –Lao Tzu

Take the First Step

If you look at various therapeutic interventions, such as CBT or the CoDA 12 Steps, you will notice that the process of healing starts with accepting your thoughts and feelings for what they are. For example, if you feel an urge to act in an improper way, acknowledge the intense emotions you are feeling and the ways in which they take over your mind and body.

Coming to the point of acceptance is never easy because you are required to come face-to-face with yourself—and when you stop running and take the time to examine yourself, who knows what horrors you might uncover? You may desire healing like anybody else but not feel comfortable shining a spotlight on your pain. Nobody is ever ready for the confrontational aspect of acceptance, the part where you have to swallow your pride and strip yourself down to a vulnerable state.

Acceptance is about seeing your reality for what it is, not what you hope it would become. But since reality isn't always pleasant, there will be times when accepting the truth will be difficult. For instance, you may find it challenging to accept the truth about the impacts of your childhood on your current relationships. You may even struggle to see your parents as less than the perfect people you have made them out to be in your mind. Accepting the truth also forces you to come to terms with past mistakes and the consequences thereof, which you may still be living with today.

But as bitter as acceptance can sometimes be, consider the suffering caused by not accepting your reality. The equivalent of not accepting reality would be to push down, block out, or downplay your thoughts and emotions. Where do those unwanted thoughts and emotions go after you have run them off? Do they magically disappear? The harsh reality is that they continue to linger below the surface, on a subconscious level, and inform the patterns of thoughts and behaviors you adopt later.

That unprocessed anger toward your parents or an ex-partner that bubbles up out of nowhere? Well, it isn't random and it isn't a coincidence. Your anger is still very much alive and active in your subconscious mind—so much so that it is one of the emotions that drives your decision-making and self-destructive behaviors. The same can be said about any other strong unprocessed emotions that you tend to push down, block out, or downplay.

Codependency issues are probably not something you want to think about every day. However, interacting with different people on a daily basis is bound to trigger your codependency issues. Therefore, what's the point of ignoring issues that are likely to cause stress and send your mind spinning on a recurring basis? Wouldn't it be helpful—as uncomfortable as it may feel—to confront your codependency issues, once and for all?

The only way out of suffering is through the gates of healing, and the only way through the gates of healing is to accept that you have codependency issues that meddle with your ability to relate with others. In this chapter, we will look at two alternative forms of therapy that can be administered at home, which can help you reach the point of acceptance.

Confront the Shadow

Psychoanalyst Carl Jung came up with a concept known as the "shadow self," which describes a dark aspect of the human unconscious mind that influences the psyche (Perry, 2022). What makes the shadow self dark is that it represents the parts of you that are difficult to accept. For instance, your shadow might represent immoral thoughts, emotional triggers, past failures, and self-destructive behaviors. In essence, everything that you push down or deny about your identity or past life experiences is hidden in your shadow.

Jung believed that part of the process of healing involved confronting your shadow self and accepting those things about your life that are difficult to admit or come to terms with. This would help to integrate your shadow into your whole identity, so you can embrace every aspect of who you are—including the dark side of your personality. The form of therapy used to confront the shadow is known as shadow work. It is a type of alternative healing intervention that requires challenging your inner critical thoughts, observing your behaviors without judgment, and accepting the reality of who you are.

What makes shadow work tough is that the focus is primarily on healing past trauma, emotional triggers, and acts of self-sabotage. Most of your fears, insecurities, or projections stem from painful situations that occurred (and were never addressed) in the past. For example, your codependency issues are not triggered by what is currently happening in your relationships but, instead, what happened many years ago that you are still trying to process and heal from.

If you simply based present moment experiences on present moment information, you wouldn't feel triggered to cling onto others, forfeit your boundaries, or choke up when it is time to assert your needs. But the past is still very much influential in how you show up and react to present moment experiences, which means that unless you heal those past wounds, they will continue to wreak havoc in your life.

Accepting the dark side of you means that you make peace with yourself and adopt a more realistic understanding about who you are. In other words, you move away from thinking that you are only good or only bad or that you can never outgrow certain habits, and you start seeing your life as a journey of highs and lows that lead you toward personal development.

Steps to Practice Shadow Work

Have you ever heard of the saying, "Hurt people, hurt people"? When you ignore the signs to heal your shadow, you may project your pain onto others or turn the attack inward and treat yourself poorly. The benefit of shadow work is that you learn to accept every part of your being—even the parts that you are currently ashamed of. The expectation of being a perfect human being is shattered, and you begin to accept the fact that you will make mistakes, offend others, or sabotage your own efforts at healing.

The goal of shadow work is to practice pausing and observing the urge, fear, or trigger—without making any judgments—and accept the experience you are having. Repeating this simple sequence over and over again is how you begin to integrate the shadow self into your whole identity.

Some of the signs that you are the perfect candidate for shadow work include

- poor self-esteem

- self-harm
- denial
- deceiving others
- self-sabotage
- inflated ego
- trouble maintaining relationships

It is important not to look at shadow work as a humiliating process where you put every dark secret on the table or force yourself to recall memories that you are not ready to face. Shadow work is about self-acceptance but also compassion. This means only going as deep into the past as you are comfortable to go and taking as long as you need before you eventually embrace your full shadow self.

Below are some of the steps you can practice to start shadow work.

Practice Noticing Your Inner Critical Thoughts

There are many ways in which your shadow self makes its presence felt. One of them is through your prevalent inner critical thoughts. Even though speaking down to yourself is normalized in society, it is often a sign of inner conflict: one aspect of you is at war with another aspect of you, which creates the back and forth insults and criticism. Paying attention to your inner critical thoughts can give you valuable insight into what the inner conflict is about and which aspects of yourself you find difficult to accept.

For a week, practice noticing and writing down every inner critical thought that you have. Don't try to analyze your thoughts or correct them in your head. Simply write down whatever you hear in your mind. At the end of the week, look at your list of inner critical thoughts and identify recurring themes, fears, or stories that emerge.

For example, are your inner critical thoughts based on physical attributes, cognitive challenges, or insecurities about your competence? These recurring patterns will reveal areas of your life (or aspects of yourself) that you find difficult to accept. You can make it your mission to work on healing each area, one at a time, through meditation, journaling, or formal counseling.

Practice the Mirror Technique to Identify Emotional Triggers

When you look into a mirror, what do you see? You see the reflection of yourself. The mirror technique can be an eye-opening exercise to notice when you are emotionally triggered and projecting your thoughts and feelings onto others. To practice mirroring, be observant of your thoughts, emotions, and body sensations during interactions with others. Notice how you feel walking into a conversation, during the exchange, and when you part ways.

Whenever you sense a negative experience, usually in the form of tightness, discomfort, or avoidance, take a moment to consider how much of the experience comes from inside of you versus how much is feedback from the other person. Ask yourself inside your head, *Is this thought or feeling mine, or feedback from the other person?* Think about whether the thought sounds like something you would think or whether the emotion is a typical trigger that you would experience in that particular situation.

Take ownership of what is yours and release anything that isn't yours. After the interaction, journal about how you felt and what might have triggered you. You can even provide a detailed description of how the trigger unfolded, so you are able to recognize situations that make you feel uncomfortable.

Practice Rethinking What Is Unacceptable

Most of what you learn to be acceptable or unacceptable about yourself is modeled in childhood. For instance, how your parents spoke to you, challenged you, or embraced your imperfections taught you how to relate to yourself. If you were raised by critical, controlling, or manipulative parents, you may have grown up believing hurtful thoughts about who you are or feeling ashamed of parts of you that your parents found difficult to accept.

Shadow work gives you an opportunity to go back in time and challenge what you were taught about yourself, specifically the negative beliefs and messages that you accepted to be true as a child. Through meditation, go back to your childhood and reflect on core memories of being judged, talked down to, yelled at, dismissed, or ridiculed.

Focus on what was said to you or implied in those moments. Challenge the messages you received by asking yourself the following questions: Were those words and criticisms fair, realistic, and loving? Did those words or criticisms match the reality of the situation? Were they warranted or exaggerations?

Through the same meditative exercise, continue to explore aspects of yourself that you struggle to accept. Think back to your earliest memory of these personal issues propping up: recall where you were, who you were with, what was being spoken or implied, and so on. Thereafter, challenge whether those things you find unacceptable are genuinely unacceptable.

For example, if you find it difficult to accept that you are a sensitive person because of being teased for being sensitive as a kid, challenge whether your sensitivity is genuinely unacceptable. Ask yourself, *Am I hurting anyone by being sensitive? Does it harm my well-being?* Continue the exercise, pulling up different kinds of qualities or behaviors that make you feel ashamed and challenge your perceptions.

Nurture Your Inner Child

The second alternative therapy that also requires a deep-dive into the past is called inner child healing. Carl

Jung is often credited for coming up with the concept of an inner child. In his list of Jungian archetypes that explore universal human patterns, he included the archetype of the child (Jacobson, 2017).

The child represents those qualities within you that are reminiscent of youth, innocence, creativity, and playfulness. Whenever you feel liberated, spontaneous, or passionate about something, you have awakened your inner child. But, of course, not every childhood memory or experience is pleasant. It is possible to grow up with a wounded inner child and, instead of being liberated, creative, or passionate, you display signs of impulsivity, dependence, rebellion, and ignorance.

In most cases, children raised in dysfunctional environments spend a good portion of their childhood in survival mode. They quickly learn that it isn't safe to express how they feel, be playful and creative, or explore the world. Many of the struggles they face are bottled inside, only to come up later when they are grown adults.

When they seek to connect to their spontaneous and creative side later on in life, they sense a disconnect due to the many years of numbing and holding back who they are. Other problems that may occur in adulthood include having trouble recognizing unmet needs, self-regulating, and problem-solving.

A wounded inner child is a child who wasn't validated, nurtured, or protected. A major sign that you could have a wounded inner child is if you were raised in an unstable and insecure family or community. Your basic needs as a child were unfulfilled, which triggered stress and anxiety. However, due to the lack of reliable support and affection, you didn't have anyone to help you process what you were going through.

Below are additional signs of having a wounded inner child. Go through the list and see how many of the signs you can resonate with:

- people-pleasing
- overworking
- obsession with success
- substance abuse problems
- unhealthy relationship patterns
- low self-esteem
- tendency to avoid conflict
- physical health issues

Other ways that the wounded inner child can manifest itself is through negative beliefs about yourself and the world around you. Here are a few beliefs that indicate you may be living with a wounded inner child:

- "There is something inherently wrong with me."
- "I am ashamed of who I am."

- "I can't trust anybody."

- "Everyone disappoints me eventually."

- "If people really knew me they would run away."

- "I don't believe in true love."

- "I am a burden on other people."

- "The world is a dangerous place."

- "I need to look out for myself."

The purpose of inner child healing is to pay attention to your wounded inner child and respond to their pain. Remember that since much of this pain stems from childhood, it hasn't been addressed before. The more you engage with your inner child, you may be surprised to remember memories from childhood that you had already forgotten—but which your inner child still holds onto. Furthermore, you may be surprised at how much certain events that you believed were not a big deal actually impacted you.

For example, you may discover that your inner child feels a sense of rejection because of not receiving physical affection from your parents. Back then, and perhaps before you start inner child healing, this may not have seemed like a big deal. As a kid, you accepted the fact that your parents are not affectionate and that didn't seem to bother you—well, at least on a surface level. You may even find that due to not being shown physical affection as a child, you either have an insatiable need for affection (e.g., very high sex drive) or you feel deeply uncomfortable with intimacy (e.g., don't like being touched).

These and many more revelations are discovered when you connect with your inner child. The purpose of inner child healing isn't to re-traumatize you but to respond to unmet physical and emotional needs, identify harmful thinking and behavioral patterns, and take the opportunity to heal from past hurts and regain a sense of vibrancy, passion, and creativity in your life. If you feel like your inner child is crying out to you, now is the perfect time to give them your undivided attention and show compassion.

Be the Parent You Wish You Had

Inner child healing incorporates shadow work as well as reflecting on your childhood. However, the main focus is on reparenting yourself, which simply means being the parent you wish you had. In order for your inner child to heal, you must step in and acknowledge their pain, then take action. Perhaps what you were missing as a child was someone to listen to you and validate your fears or take action by creating a safe environment for you to build trust and explore your sense of self.

It is impossible to fix your inner child's problems because that would entail going back to the past and changing history. Since you cannot rewrite your childhood, you can make a promise to take care of yourself in a way that your caregivers or community couldn't when you were younger. For example, if you were often left alone as a kid, you can acknowledge how that may have affected you, explore and validate your emotions, and take action by building a positive support system that makes your inner child feel safe and affirmed.

Therefore, we can identify five steps to inner child healing that involve becoming the parent you wish you had.

Step 1: Make a Connection With Your Inner Child

The first step of inner child healing is to initiate the first contact. As the "parent," you are responsible for leaning in and making a bid for connection with your "child." How you make a connection will depend on what makes your inner child feel comfortable.

In most cases, turning to childhood activities that you enjoyed can be a great way to connect with your inner child. For example, someone who enjoyed drawing might evoke their inner child through painting, someone who enjoyed playing outside in the dirt might evoke their inner child through gardening, or someone who loved playing with cars might evoke their inner child by watching a car show.

Step 2: Acknowledge Your Inner Child

After you have made a connection with your inner child, you will notice a shift in your mood and countenance, such as feeling lighter and energized. This is the best time to start a conversation with your inner child and spend time journeying into the past. But first, you must acknowledge that they exist and matter. Remember that your inner child isn't as confident, well-spoken, and mature as you are today. On a psychological level, they are also still living in the pain from the past.

Therefore, when acknowledging your inner child, imagine you are speaking to the shy, insecure, threatened little boy or girl who didn't think it was possible to survive their childhood experiences. Approach your inner child with gentleness and kindness, realizing that being shown this amount of affection may be something new for them. Reciting positive affirmations to yourself like *I am important* and *I am strong* can make your inner child feel seen and accepted. Other useful exercises include journaling about a core childhood memory (positive or negative) or visualizing a warm and loving light protecting your younger self.

Step 3: Listen to Your Inner Child

At this stage, you have connected to your inner child and acknowledged their existence. The third step is to create an emotionally safe space for your inner child to bring up whatever idea, thought, belief, feeling, or memory that they wish to share. It is important to allow your inner child to lead this exercise and be open to accept whatever they choose to share on that particular day.

For example, sometimes when you connect with your inner child, they may want to have a light encounter where you recall a positive memory and enjoy pleasurable emotions. When this happens, you should go with the flow instead of trying to redirect your inner child's focus to something else. Even though your inner child may be wounded, they won't want to delve into deep and sensitive topics all of the time. Like any child, they may want to play and have fun more than doing the "serious stuff."

Exercises that can help you listen to your inner child are meditation and journaling. During a meditation practice, you can attempt to locate your inner child within yourself (you might focus on your internal thoughts or connect with your heart). Thereafter, patiently wait for something to come up. Avoid pre-empting what that "something" will be. Just enjoy your own company and continue taking deep breaths until your inner child decides to speak.

If you decide to practice journaling, you can use journal prompts to encourage your inner child to speak. These prompts could be based on specific topics or generalized to allow your inner child to direct the interaction. Below are some examples of prompts you can use to get the conversation started:

- How are you today?

- What is on your mind?

- How are you feeling?

- What do you need right now?

- How can I help you?

- Who are you upset with?

- What would you like to share with me?

- What do you wish you could let go of?

- What would make this moment feel better?

There are times when you will sit down to listen to your inner child and they may not have anything to say. When this happens, thank your inner child for spending time with you and cut the meditation or journal practice short. Try to avoid probing or forcing something to come out. Remember that you are striving to become a parent that you wish you had, so do your best to practice gentle and loving behaviors, like respecting your inner child's choices.

There will also be times when your inner child has so much to say, which cannot be processed within a single meditation or journaling session. In this case, you may need to step in and offer more structure to the conversation, such as asking your inner child to focus on one subject, one memory, or one specific individual they wish to bring up. Reassure them that you will give them an opportunity to share all of their thoughts and feelings in the following sessions. If you are meditating, it may be useful to keep a pen and notepad next to you, so you can jot down what you heard after your session is complete.

Step 4: Validate Your Inner Child

Take a few moments to appreciate the courage it took for your inner child to share what was on their mind. If you are aware of experiencing issues expressing your opinions as a child, being able to speak up is a big milestone!

The fourth step of inner child healing is about validating what you heard. Whether the information received from your inner child was silly or something to be taken seriously, let them know that you value what they have to say. There are different ways to express this important message.

The first would be saying loudly to yourself, *I hear you* or *What you are saying makes sense to me*. If your inner child has shared something humorous, you could smile or laugh. You could also visualize yourself (older self) entering the setting of the childhood memory (e.g., revisiting your childhood home) and sitting next to your younger self during a stressful or traumatic incident (e.g., during a heated argument between your parents).

When validating your inner child, remember to focus on accepting the reality of what they may be thinking or feeling, rather than trying to solve the problem. Your job as the parent is to make your inner child feel comfortable sharing both pleasant and unpleasant experiences with you, without feeling scared about how you might respond. They should be able to trust that even when you don't understand the "why," you are still a reliable source of support.

Step 5: Take Action on Behalf of Your Inner Child

This final step is not always appropriate or necessary; therefore, you will need to assess whether to take action on a case-by-case basis. For example, there will be times when your inner child shares information that requires you to stand in the gap and do something. This could be after your inner child has expressed an unmet emotional need or asked for assistance healing from a childhood situation. Taking action is important to establish trust and help your inner child heal.

However, there will also be times when your inner child shares feelings about a past event or comments about what they thought when a specific situation was happening. Both of these instances don't require taking action, apart from validating your inner child's experiences. If you are not sure whether to take action or not, you can also ask your inner child for guidance and get a sense of how they would like for you to respond.

The type of action you take will also differ based on what was shared. To avoid disappointing your inner child, always keep the expectations for taking action low. In other words, commit to a task that is small and manageable, something that won't require you to journey too far out of your comfort zone. Similar to how you would approach any child, avoid making promises that are difficult to keep.

These five steps, repeated over and over again, will help you start and continue the process of healing your inner child. Along the way, your codependency issues may be brought up and you will get opportunities to heal from those patterns too! The best part of inner child healing, however, is that you are able to go beyond codependency and heal from other dysfunctional patterns learned from childhood. Therefore, go into this process with an open mind and plenty of time on your hands.

Chapter 8:

Break Free From Codependent Loving Relationships

Allowing others to suffer the consequences of their own actions, without enabling them, is the best motivation for them to undertake the difficult task of change. –Darlene Lancer

What Do Codependent Friendships and Romantic Relationships Look Like?

All codependent relationships consist of a giver-taker dynamic. This is no different in codependent friendships or romantic relationships. One person takes on the role of a self-sacrificing giver, who is overly concerned about the needs of the other person—the taker. In many cases, the taker portrays themselves as someone who is always in crisis or needs support. The giver feels compelled to rescue them out of these crises and show their undying loyalty.

What makes this type of dynamic unhealthy is the imbalance of power. For instance, the giver is always overextending themselves, while the taker is always on the receiving end of support. There isn't enough reciprocity in the relationship to ensure that both people are getting their needs met and feeling cherished.

It can be difficult spotting a codependency pattern when someone you care about is going through a difficult time. It is natural to want to show up for a friend or partner who has recently suffered a terrible experience or maybe lives with unaddressed trauma. However, the difference between a healthy relationship and a codependent one can be summarized in one word—boundaries.

Due to the lack of boundaries, a codependent friend or partner doesn't know when to set limits and bow out. They give and give and give until they feel physically, mentally, and emotionally exhausted. But even after reaching their breaking point, a codependent friend or partner will continue to stress about the well-being of the other person and feel guilty when they cannot physically do anything to help. Below are some of the signs of a codependent friendship or romantic relationship, based on the giver-taker roles:

- The taker is always in a crisis and needs to be rescued; the giver feels a deep sense of responsibility to provide a solution.

- The taker needs a lot of reassurance to feel happy; the giver provides ongoing emotional support.

- The taker is independent and is comfortable going days without checking in; the giver feels anxious when they don't hear back from their friend.

- The taker feels positive about the friendships; the giver feels burned out but tries to hide it.

- The taker enjoys talking about themselves and how they feel; the giver struggles to share their thoughts and emotions freely.

- The taker feels comfortable when they receive attention from their friend; the giver prefers to fade in the background and allow their friend to have the spotlight.

- The taker would happily live without their friend if the situation called for it; the giver feels anxious thinking about life without their friend.

These are broad examples of what codependency in loving relationships might look like. Your dynamic could be more complex based on unique circumstances; however, it will most likely follow one or all of the patterns mentioned.

What's in It for You?

When we look at codependency in friendships or romantic relationships, we can sometimes feel sorry for the giver, who to us, appears to be getting in the short end of the stick. But the truth is that although there is a power imbalance, both the giver and the taker get something out of the union.

From the outside looking in, it is obvious to see what the taker gets out of the relationship: They have a friend or partner who is physically, mentally, and emotionally tuned in to their needs. But the giver gets some type of indirect reward, too. Since they desire to be needed by others, they feel a boost of confidence and sense of importance when they are depended on. Whenever they are required to show up for their friend or partner, they jump at the opportunity because by sacrificing their time, money, and energy, they walk away feeling validated by the experience.

For example, the giver might become friends with a self-centered taker who only cares about what they can get out of the friendship. Perhaps what drew the taker to the giver was their lack of boundaries, which allowed them to get away with disrespectful behavior. On the other hand, the giver recognizes that their friend isn't the most attentive or patient person. But despite the drawbacks outweighing the opportunities, the giver continues to maintain friendship. While this friendship isn't reciprocal, the giver feels important whenever they are hanging around the taker. It's almost like they "borrow" confidence from the self-absorbed friend and feel good in their company.

Of course, there are consequences to not having boundaries with friends or romantic partners. Even though the giver feels good about themselves for going above and beyond for their significant other, they will reach a point where it stops making practical sense to keep pouring into them without reciprocation. If they choose to ignore the signs to stop giving and take a step back, they can become more enmeshed and entangled in this unhealthy relationship pattern. When the relationship ends, the only person who will walk away feeling physically and emotionally drained is the one who failed to prioritize their own well-being for the sake of receiving external validation.

If you discover that you may be friends or partnered with someone who doesn't reciprocate or respect your boundaries, think about what you are getting out of the relationship. In most cases, there is a core need that is validated which keeps you going back to them.

Strategies to Break Free From Codependent Friendships and Romantic Relationships

It is possible to address codependency issues within a friendship or romantic relationship without having to cut ties with the other person. Whenever you are caught in a codependency cycle with a friend or partner, the following strategies will help you break free.

Take Ownership of Where You Went Wrong

Look at yourself in the mirror and be honest about your role in creating this relationship dynamic. Consider how you became the giver, particularly the behaviors you performed repeatedly to make the other person dependent on you. You can also reflect on the satisfaction you get from being a giver and explore where that satisfaction stems from.

Taking the time to assess your situation from an honest place can help you identify recurring habits that draw you to certain people or cause you to experience the same unhealthy relationships. When you know what you are doing wrong, you get a chance to address your problems and break the pattern.

Create a List of Values That Matter to You in a Friendship

Now that you have a sober understanding of the mistakes you could be making in the relationship, think deeply about what a wholesome and nurturing friendship or romantic relationship means and looks like for you. It is common for codependent people to focus on responding to other people's needs and neglect their own needs in the process. Now is the time to zone in on what you look for in a good friend or partner so that you are able to set standards for your relationships.

One way to do this is to create a list of values that matter most to you in both types of relationships.

Think about the qualities you admire in a good friend or partner, the nature of your relationship, and how you show up for each other. Write down your list of values on a piece of paper. Keep your list as a reminder of what you expect, moving forward, from your friend.

Here is a short list of values to help you get started:

- honesty
- kindness
- empathy
- curiosity
- acceptance
- intelligence
- humor
- adventure
- support
- loyalty
- open communication

Set Healthy Boundaries and Consequences

In Chapter 5, we spoke about the signs of low self-worth and mentioned weak or rigid boundaries as one of them. In codependent friendships or romantic relationships, it is common to find weak boundaries where the giver sets rules but doesn't enforce them or follow through with consequences. Learning how to set and enforce healthy boundaries can help you adjust the power imbalance in your relationships and offer you more control over your time and efforts.

An easy way to learn how to set healthy boundaries is to practice the DESC method of conflict resolution. This method includes four steps to communicating boundaries and consequences whenever you feel the need to set a limit with a friend or partner (i.e., when you notice a lack of reciprocation, inconsiderate behaviors, offensive behaviors). This method is non-confrontational, which makes it suitable for you if you tend to avoid conflict.

Below are the steps to practice DESC (Anderson, 2018).

D = Describe the Behavior Objectively

Describe the behavior that has made you feel the need to set a limit. Focus on the action that took place, and try to describe it objectively. Consider what happened, where it took place, who was there, and how the action unfolded. Leave out your opinions or the emotional impact it had on you—you will get a chance to express your feelings in the following step.

Example: *Earlier today, when we spoke on the phone, you didn't ask me how I was doing. The conversation was centered around your day and the concerns you were having.*

E = Express How It Made You Feel

Explain how the behavior made you feel. Here, you can openly share your subjective experience. Your aim should be to describe how you felt so that the other person gets an opportunity to step inside your shoes. Remember to use "I" statements rather than "you" statements to keep the focus on your unique experience. Plus, you don't want to make the other person feel guilty or responsible for something you felt inside.

Example: *I felt annoyed because I was doing my best to listen and validate what you were saying, but I felt you couldn't do the same for me. I also felt taken for granted for giving so much and not getting any positive reinforcement in return.*

S = Specify What You Need Moving Forward

At this stage of the conversation, you can set a boundary by specifying what you need from the other person moving forward. Note that as soon as you set the boundary, there will be an expectation for them to honor your need. For instance, if you ask for something, like empathy, they will be expected to provide it whenever a similar situation occurs. On the other hand, if you ask the person to stop doing something, like to stop hogging conversations, they will be expected to be mindful of when they are committing that behavior and voluntarily check themselves.

When specifying what you need, be considerate of the other person's rights and needs. Avoid asking for behavior that pushes them too far out of their comfort zone. In general, your boundary should be something that doesn't require the other person to overextend themselves. To test whether your boundary is appropriate, think about how you would feel if someone made a similar request to you.

Example: *Moving forward, may you please be mindful of when the conversation is not balanced? For example, after you have shared something, may you please turn the conversation back to me by asking a question and hearing what I have to say?*

C=Create a Consequence or Compromise

Lastly, it is critical to explain the consequences for not honoring the boundary. The purpose of this is to show the other person how serious you are about having your needs met as well as to give them an idea of how you may react when a similar offense occurs in the future. Consequences are not supposed to be used as punishment, so avoid anything that might hurt the other person. The goal of consequences is to reinforce good behaviors by taking action whenever bad behaviors happen.

Some situations may not call for consequences but rather a compromise. For example, you may want the other person to meet you halfway by adjusting their behaviors slightly. Be open to discussing the compromise and coming up with a solution that works for both of you. If you have already decided to create a consequence, there is no room for compromising (i.e., it is either they honor your boundary or face the consequence).

Example: *If the same situation happens in future, I will have no other option but to cut the conversation short and drop the call because the exchange is not reciprocal.*

Healthy boundaries are fair and balanced. They are created to protect you from exploitation or mistreatment while also being mindful of the other person. Healthy boundaries can help you advocate for your needs without overstepping your friend's or partner's boundaries. In essence, they seek to create a win-win situation where both parties' rights are respected and the relationship can flourish in a safe and reciprocal environment.

Chapter 9:

Break Free From Codependent Work Relationships

When we care too much for a person that doesn't care at all, we lose ourselves. Never again should you allow to not be given to equally. –Tracy A Malone

What Do Codependent Work Relationships Look Like?

Sometimes codependency doesn't manifest within friendships or romantic relationships but instead at work. Similar to other codependent relationship dynamics, codependent work relationships are characterized by an imbalance of power. It occurs between one employee or employer who is extremely demanding and another coworker who struggles to stand up for themselves or feels overly responsible for the success of the team.

A codependent employee is usually disempowered. They have developed a habit of sidelining their own needs in order to please coworkers (or a specific coworker). This is born out of a belief that sacrificing their time and energy at work (more than is required from them) will be rewarding in the long run. For instance, a codependent employee might think that being always ready to take on more work could land them a promotion in the future or cause them to earn the respect of their manager. Beliefs like these are what motivate them to continue overextending themselves.

Other common signs of a codependent employee include

- being agreeable to avoid confrontation or debate of ideas
- frequently asking their manager or coworkers for permission to carry out simple tasks
- apologizing for behavior that isn't their fault or common mistakes that don't require an apology
- taking on more work than they can handle and feeling overwhelmed later
- seeking regular praise from their manager to feel confident in their abilities

What codependent employees don't realize is that being too available and flexible doesn't win coworkers over; it makes them vulnerable to being abused or manipulated. For example, when a coworker learns that you are willing to say yes to any work request, they can contact you after hours with work-related matters, assign you to challenging projects that you aren't capable of handling, or attempt to control your workflow. Moreover, since they have picked up that you tend to be passive with authority, they may continue to harass you knowing that you are less likely to take action against them.

What About Codependent Managers?

A codependent manager is also overly invested in their work relationships but in a different way. While they are hard workers, who are often very successful at what they do, they can also be guilty of micromanaging their team. Due to over-functioning and having high standards for themselves and others, they will frequently cross boundaries, edit team members' work without their permission, and compensate for any deficits in the team by taking on more duties. Under a codependent manager, it is very difficult for employees to develop their competencies and grow into leaders. The manager may want to be looped in every task and have the final say about the quality of a project.

The consequences of over-functioning are that it can lead to anxiety, meltdowns, and burnout. It is simply impossible to be everything to everyone at the office, without reaching a breaking point. If you are a codependent manager, you have probably fallen ill on several occasions due to work stress or run into power struggles with your team members.

Your obsessive need to be recognized at work may have even taken a toll on your self-esteem. For instance, you may feel undervalued when your employees don't depend on you for assistance or when you are given constructive criticism. On the one hand, you want to be everyone's favorite manager, but, on the other hand, you struggle to see your employees as unique individuals who have separate goals and desires from you.

Strategies to Break Free From Codependent Work Relationships

When seeking to break free from codependent work relationships, the first step is to figure out what types of codependency issues you display at work. Depending on whether you are a codependent employee or manager, you will exhibit different kinds of codependent behaviors.

The second step is to trace the root of your codependency issues. Are they issues you have dealt with your whole life, which manifest in other types of relationships, too? Or could they be issues that began at work? What many professionals are unaware of is that codependency can be a result of a toxic work culture, where a company is controlled by a taker (usually the CEO) and all of the employees are organized and assigned roles based on the owner's needs and desires.

In these types of workplaces, it is rare to find company values and traditions that unite workers. What's common are arbitrary rules and nonsensical procedures that are designed to limit the growth potential of employees and discourage collaboration. Instead of working toward mutual goals, employees strive to make the CEO happy. There are also few to no systems put in place to create clear boundaries and hold employees (including the CEO) accountable for their actions.

If you ever find yourself working in this type of workplace, you may also be exposed to workplace abuse and discrimination. Whenever there are poor boundaries, employees and managers are vulnerable to being exploited, targeted, and harassed. If leaving the company is not an option, there are other strategies that you can practice to break free from the codependent culture enforced at work.

Establish Work Boundaries

Whether your codependency issues stem from personal experiences or a toxic work culture, you can benefit from setting work boundaries. Like normal personal boundaries, work boundaries establish healthy limits in a professional environment and set the tone for your work relationships.

Remember that the shortest and most effective boundary is the word *no*. However, depending on how you would like to structure your work life, there are additional boundaries you can establish, such as

1. **Physical boundaries**: These are related to your level of comfortability having others enter your personal space. These could include boundaries about your workstation, personal space, and appropriate (or inappropriate) touching with coworkers.

2. **Emotional boundaries**: These boundaries can help you separate your emotional experience from a coworker's emotional experience. They may include things like refusing to accept blame for something you haven't done, expressing to your manager when and how you would like to receive feedback, or saying no to extra work or requests made at short notice.

3. **Mental boundaries**: These boundaries are created to support your mental well-being at work and ensure you are able to enjoy a good work-life balance. These types of boundaries revolve around your use of time (e.g., establishing work hours), taking breaks or time off work, not being roped into office politics, and protecting your right to express your opinions or concerns.

Avoid Internalizing Negative Messages

You will come across different types of people at work. Some may be kind and others may be self-centered. There will also be a few coworkers who are hellbent on misunderstanding you or who make it difficult to work together in harmony. As a codependent person, your initial approach may be to be on good terms with everybody to avoid conflict. However, when there are members on your team who are not motivated to work peacefully, they will find ways to cause drama.

To protect yourself from their insults or microaggressions, it is important to teach yourself not to internalize every negative message you receive from others. For example, if somebody dislikes you, avoid the temptation to think you are not a good person. Or when you are the victim of bullying at work, avoid the temptation to think that the abuse has something to do with your personal flaws or weaknesses. There is no excuse to justify the negative attitudes or behaviors of coworkers. Furthermore, their toxic energy isn't anything that you can fix or change by being more selfless and kind.

Practice the mirror technique (refer back to Chapter 7) and examine how much of the recurring conflict or tension has to do with your attitudes and behaviors and how much of it was caused by other people. Only accept what you are responsible for and refuse to take on unnecessary blame.

Limit Engagements With Toxic Coworkers

Do you remember our discussion about loving detachment? There will be times at work where you will need to lovingly detach from coworkers who refuse to participate in efforts of conflict resolution. For some coworkers, the only way they can learn to give you the respect you deserve is if you create physical and mental distance. In other words, limit your engagement to strictly work-related matters and avoid conversations outside of those parameters.

When they insist on roping you into work conflict, rely on company mediators and policies to resolve work issues. It may also be useful to document your interactions through emails so you have proof of your exchanges in case they try to spin lies or blackmail you. It is important to remember that the biggest nemesis of a codependent individual in the workplace is a narcissistic coworker—and workplaces tend to have many narcissists seeking to lie, cheat, and create chaos for others.

Conclusion

We will martyr ourselves, suffering under the weight of a non-reciprocal relationship until some part of us bursts in protest. —
Mary Crocker Cook

Codependency is an unhealthy relationship pattern that has many different faces, meaning that it can stem from various factors and experiences. When the concept of codependency was first introduced, we knew it as a condition that only affects family members of addicts. However, today we know that codependency can affect anybody, at any stage of life, triggered by various traumas.

Since codependency is not a medical disorder, it can be treated through psychotherapeutic interventions, such as CBT, meditation, journaling, shadow work, and inner child healing. Joining communities of like-minded people, like Codependents Anonymous, can be another way to heal codependency and learn how to build healthy and mutually satisfying relationships.

What is important to remember about codependency is that the pattern stems from a deep emotional wound, which is the fear of abandonment. Knowing and accepting this can help you identify emotional triggers that cause you to latch onto other people and fear being separated from them. Of course, identifying these emotional triggers is only the beginning of your healing journey. Nevertheless, the sooner you accept that you may be living with the fear of abandonment, the sooner you can start confronting the underlying issues.

Whether your codependent behaviors began in the womb, after the first big relationship breakup, or many years of working at a toxic workplace, the takeaway message for you is that healing is possible. You are capable of breaking free from the destructive cycle of codependency and teaching yourself how to relate to others in healthier ways.

But even better than breaking free from codependency, you are capable of using the exercises and techniques mentioned in this book to rebuild your sense of self and develop a solid identity separate from other people. There is still so much of who you are that is yet to be explored and embraced. Healing from codependency gives you an opportunity to invest in the most important relationship in your life, which is the relationship you have with yourself!

If you have learned something new about yourself while reading this book, share your experience and leave a review on Amazon!

About the Author

Cameron J. Clark, MSW, MFCC, is a dedicated life coach, passionate about empowering women who have experienced abusive relationships or struggle with low self-esteem and self-love. Drawing from her personal journey of overcoming an unhappy and abusive past, Cameron has transformed her life and is now happily thriving in a loving relationship.

With her compassionate and empathetic approach, she is committed to helping others find their inner strength, rebuild their confidence, and create healthy, fulfilling relationships. Cameron's unique coaching style combines practical strategies with emotional support, enabling her clients to break free from the chains of their past and embrace a future full of hope and joy.

When she's not guiding and inspiring women to reclaim their lives, Cameron enjoys spending quality time with her loved ones and her beloved dog, Luca. An avid reader, she finds solace and inspiration in the pages of a good book. Cameron also cherishes her wine nights with friends, celebrating the beautiful bonds of sisterhood and the journey they share toward healing and self-discovery.

References

Ackerman, C. (2018, November 6). *What is self-worth and how do we increase it?* PositivePsychology. https://positivepsychology.com/self-worth/

Aion Recovery. (2021, May 17). *Five codependency and addiction family roles.* https://aionrecovery.com/articles/five-codependency-and-addiction-family-roles/

Anderson, M. (2018, January 23). *DESC: Your script for becoming more assertive.* WSCPA. https://www.wscpa.org/community/future-cpas/become-a-cpa-blog/wscpa-blog/2018/01/23/desc-your-script-for-becoming-more-assertive

Association for Psychological Science. (2011, November 10). Can fetus sense mother's psychological state? Study suggests yes. *ScienceDaily.* https://www.sciencedaily.com/releases/2011/11/111110142352.htm

Beattie, M. (n.d.). *Melody Beattie quote.* Goodreads. https://www.goodreads.com/author/show/4482.Melody_Beattie

Beecher, Henry Ward. (2022, June 3). *140 bond between mother and child quotes to warm your heart.*

Quotement. https://quotement.com/bond-between-mother-and-child-quotes/

Belle, E. (2020, May 22). *Codependency: How emotional neglect turns us into people-pleasers.* Healthline. https://www.healthline.com/health/mental-health/codependency-and-attachment-trauma

Bright Horizons. (2019, February 19). *How children develop identity.* https://www.brighthorizons.com/resources/Article/how-children-develop-identity#

Brown, B. (n.d.). *The 246 best quotes about identity.* Bookroo. https://bookroo.com/quotes/identity

Cherry, K. (2022, December 23). *What is permissive parenting?* Verywell Mind. https://www.verywellmind.com/what-is-permissive-parenting-2794957

Codependents Anonymous. (n.d.). *Twelve steps.* https://coda.org/meeting-materials/twelve-steps/

Coelho, P. (2022, March 28). *People pleaser quotes – 44 wise thoughts.* Empowered and Thriving. https://empoweredandthriving.com/people-pleaser-quotes/

Cook, M. C. (n.d.). *Mary Crocker Cook quote.* Goodreads. https://www.goodreads.com/author/show/5091051.Mary_Crocker_Cook

Dines, C. (n.d.). *Christopher Dines quote.* Goodreads. https://www.goodreads.com/author/show/5224793.Christopher_Dines

Eanes, R. (2016, January 15). *Turning toward our children: Answering bids for connection.* The Gottman Institute. https://www.gottman.com/blog/turning-toward-our-children-answering-bids-for-connection/

Family First Intervention. (2012). *Drug and alcohol addiction codependency.* https://family-intervention.com/family-roles/codependency/

Farnam Street. (2019, June 3). *The danger of comparing yourself to others.* https://fs.blog/comparing-yourself-others/

Gould, W. R. (2022, November 7). *What is codependency?* Verywell Mind. https://www.verywellmind.com/what-is-codependency-5072124

Greater Sacramento Area CoDA Community. (n.d.) *Welcome to CoDA.* http://www.greatersaccoda.org/foundational/Welcome-Packet.pdf

Gregory, M. (2019, May 7). *What does the "still face" experiment teach us about connection?* PsychHelp. https://psychhelp.com.au/what-does-the-still-face-experiment-teach-us-about-connection/

Indeed Editorial Team. (2022, September 15). *What is co-dependency in the workplace? (with common signs).* https://au.indeed.com/career-advice/career-development/co-dependency-in-work-place#

Indeed Editorial Team. (2023, March 11). *16 Ways to set healthy boundaries at work.* Indeed Career Guide. https://www.indeed.com/career-advice/career-development/boundaries-at-work

Jacobson, S. (2017, March 23). *What is the "inner child"?* Harley Therapy Blog. https://www.harleytherapy.co.uk/counselling/what-is-the-inner-child.htm

Jantz, G. L. (2018, October 30). *Codependency and emotional abuse.* PsychologyToday. https://www.psychologytoday.com/za/blog/hope-relationships/201810/codependency-and-emotional-abuse

Jones, D. M. (n.d.). *Codependency quotes (146 quotes).* Goodreads. https://www.goodreads.com/quotes/tag/codependency

Kempton, S. (2007, August 28). *The 5 stages of detachment: Learning how to let go.* Yoga Journal. https://www.yogajournal.com/yoga-101/spirituality/practice-detachment/

Lancer, D. (n.d.). *Codependency quotes (161 quotes).* Goodreads. https://www.goodreads.com/quotes/tag/codependency?page=3

Lumen Learning. (n.d.). Identity formation: Lifespan development. In *Module 7: Adolescence*. https://courses.lumenlearning.com/wm-lifespandevelopment/chapter/identity-formation/

Malone, T. A. (n.d.). *Codependency quotes (161 quotes)*. Goodreads. https://www.goodreads.com/quotes/tag/codependency?page=4

Mandriota, M. (2021, October 13). *4 types of attachment: What's your style?* Psych Central. https://psychcentral.com/health/4-attachment-styles-in-relationships#attachment-types

March of Dimes. (2023, February). *Stress and pregnancy*. https://www.marchofdimes.org/find-support/topics/pregnancy/stress-and-pregnancy

Martin, S. (2018, June 29). *Dysfunctional family dynamics: Dont talk, dont trust, dont feel*. Psych Central. https://psychcentral.com/blog/imperfect/2018/06/dysfunctional-family-dynamics-dont-talk-dont-trust-dont-feel#Dysfunctional-family-rules

Martin, S. (2020a, June 11). *How and why to detach with love*. Psych Central. https://psychcentral.com/blog/imperfect/2020/06/how-and-why-to-detach-with-love#1

Martin, S. (2020b, June 22). *Are your boundaries too weak or too rigid?* Psych Central. https://psychcentral.com/blog/imperfect/2020

/06/are-your-boundaries-too-weak-or-too-rigid#Signs-of-rigid-boundaries

Martin, S. (2020c, October 2). *5 myths about codependency.* Live Well with Sharon Martin. https://www.livewellwithsharonmartin.com/5-myths-about-codependency/

Mental Health America. (n.d.). *Co-dependency.* https://www.mhanational.org/co-dependency

Meyers, S. (2017, July 21). *The root of overprotective parenting: Codependent parents?* PsychologyToday. https://www.psychologytoday.com/za/blog/insight-is-2020/201707/the-root-overprotective-parenting-codependent-parents

Michaels, J. (2017, January 13). Issues [Song]. On *Nervous System - EP*. StarGate & Benny Blanco (Producers). Genius. https://genius.com/Julia-michaels-issues-lyrics

Moore, J. E. (n.d.). *Jennifer Elizabeth Moore quote.* Goodreads. https://www.goodreads.com/author/show/19611286.Jennifer_Elizabeth_Moore

Pedersen, T., & Smith, J. (2022, November 16). *How to heal your inner child: 10 self-soothing tips.* Psych Central. https://psychcentral.com/health/how-to-heal-your-inner-child

Perry, E. (2022, June 13). *8 benefits of shadow work and how to start practicing it.* BetterUp. https://www.betterup.com/blog/shadow-work

Pregnancy, Birth, and Baby. (2023, May). *Bonding with your baby during pregnancy*. PregnancyBirthBaby. https://www.pregnancybirthbaby.org.au/bonding-with-your-baby-during-pregnancy#

Recovery Village. (2023, May 8). *6 myths and facts about codependency and codependent relationships*. https://www.therecoveryvillage.com/mental-health/codependency/codependency-myths/

Rice, M. (2023, January 23). *Codependency in friendships: Exploring the signs*. Talkspace. https://www.talkspace.com/blog/codependency-in-friendship/#

Salters-Pedneault, K. (2022, November 14). *Why many people with BPD lack a strong sense of self*. Verywell Mind. https://www.verywellmind.com/borderline-personality-disorder-identity-issues-425488#

Solara Staff Writer. (2019, November 7). *How to heal your inner child in seven steps*. Solara Mental Health. https://solaramentalhealth.com/heal-your-inner-child/

Sparks, J., & Brown, C. (2008, February 11). No Air [Song]. On *Jordin Sparks*. The Underdogs (Producers). Genius. https://genius.com/Jordin-sparks-and-chris-brown-no-air-lyrics

Turner, S. (2018, January 9). *The parable of the elephant and the chain*. Medium. https://medium.com/@shandonsteve_71979/t

he-parable-of-the-elephant-and-the-chain-aedff7b60aea

Tzu, L. (n.d.). *Lao Tzu quote*. Goodreads. https://www.goodreads.com/author/show/2622245.Lao_Tzu

Wall, S. (2021, July 7). *How to detach with love*. Lakeside-Milam Seattle. https://lakesidemilam.com/blog/detach-with-love/

West, M. (2023, March 30). *Codependent personality: Disorder, signs, and treatment*. MedicalNewsToday. https://www.medicalnewstoday.com/articles/codependent-personality-disorder#causes

Wood, K. M. (2022, June 13). *How to treat codependency: CBT and codependency*. Confidently Authentic. https://confidentlyauthentic.com/cbt-and-codependency/

Woodward, A. (2023, May 16). *7 signs of a wounded inner child*. Kinder World. https://www.playkinderworld.com/blog/7-signs-of-a-wounded-inner-child

Wright, S. A. (2022, February 28). *Love addiction: The stages of codependency*. Psych Central. https://psychcentral.com/addictions/stages-of-codependency-love-addiction#stages-of-codependency

Made in the USA
Columbia, SC
23 October 2024